# PERSONAL RESPONSIBILITY

IS VOLUME

## 33

OF THE

Twentieth Century Encyclopedia of Catholicism

UNDER SECTION

## III

*THE NATURE OF MAN*

IT IS ALSO THE

## 111TH

VOLUME IN ORDER OF PUBLICATION

*Edited by HENRI DANIEL-ROPS of the Académie Française*

# PERSONAL RESPONSIBILITY

*By MONICA LAWLOR*

HAWTHORN BOOKS · PUBLISHERS · *New York*

*155.2*
*L P*

*First Edition,* November, 1963

NIHIL OBSTAT

Joannes M. T. Barton, S.T.D., L.S.S.

   *Censor Deputatus*

IMPRIMATUR

Georgius L. Craven

   *Episcopus Sebastopolis, Vic. Cap.*

Westmonasterii, die XVI SEPTEMBRIS MCMLXIII

H-9545

# CONTENTS

## PART II: MAN AS AN INDIVIDUAL

# INTRODUCTION

This is not a book for the professional psychologist; it is intended for those who would like to know something about what psychology has to say about the ordinary person, but who do not particularly want to read a textbook. Those who already have some knowledge of the subject may find the end of the book of some interest as it is less obviously derivative than the earlier part. While this is in no sense a textbook, where possible there are references to original work that seems to me interesting; this is so that people can have a chance to take a closer look at the evidence on any point that interests or annoys them, if they feel that way inclined.

The general theme of the book has been chosen because it could interest many people; the problem of responsibility and freedom affects us all closely and is something about which, in one way or another, psychologists have had a good deal to say. It seems fair, then, that psychologists should from time to time make the effort to explain to people just what evidence and theory they base their pronouncements upon; so that people can decide how much of it all they want to take seriously.

With this end in view, what I have tried to do is to outline in a brief, and often I am afraid, fragmentary way the things which make us what we are.

The first part of the book deals with man as a species, that is, it is an attempt to say something of the characteristics which our human heredity imposes upon us; this means discussing the way we know the world around us and the way in which our experience is patterned and formed by our nature. It then goes on to deal with the main ways in which culture, and the necessities of human life in society, both form and control us. All men are born into society and that, with the physical fact of humanity, is our inescapable heritage.

The second part of the book concentrates on the differences that make us individuals as well as men, and on the organization of the particular person. This part starts with a discussion of individual differences in heredity and ends with an analysis of choice. This is because I believe that choice is central to the whole idea of self-determination and personal freedom.

The general idea is that the book should move from those dispositions and limitations which are virtually inescapable, to the core of individuality which makes sense of the idea that we can choose between good and evil. It may seem on balance that more has been said about determinants than freedom, but that is not only because we see the one more clearly in the face of the other, but also because in so much we are alike, even to the point of being alike in the way in which we can be different. Psychology has more to do with general principles or modes of operation, and less with the specific content of actions than is commonly realized.

The last part of the book is an attempt to draw together the threads and to state as clearly as possible what can be said of human moral freedom. In this postscript I have discussed some of the more important "determinist" views of psychology in order to explore the limits of their validity.

One over-riding consideration will be assumed in what follows: that the individual is never at any time a sort of passive biological blotting paper upon which experiences register. The idea of man at birth as a *tabula rasa* is inaccurate, not so much because it presupposes no mental content, but because it suggests a degree of passivity which is totally at variance with even the mental life of a rabbit. Rabbits no less than people interpret and organize their experience because in some degree they must, although they clearly do not have the same quality of organization or interpretation. To many psychologists any such idea is a mystical heresy, but it is not *a priori* more ridiculous than the respectable assumption that animals are machines, and it explains many features of animal and human behaviour a good deal better. This then, is a bias, but whether it ultimately derives from my interest in animals, my Christianity or the sheer force of the evidence, I will leave the reader to decide.

One last word, and that of warning. There are no easy answers to the interesting questions of psychology, and if in what follows I suggest that psychological theory is conflicting and confused, that is only half the story—though real enough. The important thing is that the questions have begun to become clear and the relative strengths and weaknesses of the different theories that are discussed do centre around questions we can answer at least in part. These answers immediately pose new questions, but that is to be expected. Gross oversimplification can make a popular treatment of theory in other sciences look "tight" and complete; such attempts in psychology are an obvious mistake; unless couched in quite unintelligible jargon, they invite the reader to a justified criticism based on his own experience. While the untrained person may often make quite false assumptions about himself and others, and be bitterly resistant to and scornful of unpalatable theories about human nature, a theory which rings false or trite will not satisfy him for long because experience will repeatedly fail to verify it. So that where confusion reigns and theories conflict, I have tried to make this clear; it may make the book more difficult to read but simplicity can be bought at too high a price.

This book has been written largely because I believe that psychology has, in the present century, changed our idea of the nature of man; this imposes on the professional psychologist a responsibility for making the theories and findings of psychology accessible to those who are inevitably influenced in some measure by their ideas. The slant of the book is towards a proper understanding of psychological determinism, because it is particularly our notion of personal responsibility which has been affected by psychology. What I have attempted is to put some perspective on the often categorical statements about human freedom and determinism which may irritate, bewilder or bewitch the ordinary man.

The psychology here discussed is not specifically "Christian"; it is merely as straightforward an account of the relevant aspects of that science as I can manage. This may disappoint some people, but I do not myself believe that any distinction of this kind is meaningful. My hope is that, by making use of the findings of current psychology to approach what is both a theological and a psychological problem, I may have been able to show that it is possible for an interesting and fruitful interaction of these two disciplines to take place in the modern world, in the language of that world, although such a dialogue is beyond the scope of this book.

Bedford College,
June 1963.

# PART I

# THE NATURE OF MAN

# CHAPTER I

# MAN AS A SPECIES

## THE PATTERNING OF BEHAVIOUR

### Our common heredity

Our physical and psychological make-up is largely accounted for by inheritance; we are what we are with two hands, two feet, two eyes—with taste, hearing, smell and speech, with our experience of the world limited by both our sensory make-up and our muscular organization, because of the genetic pattern of our species. We are built so that we can add to our knowledge by thinking, but we can experience directly only in certain given ways. Since species differ in sensory endowment we can come to a secondhand knowledge of somewhat different ways of experiencing the world; we can, through a range of instruments and techniques (such as the microscope and radio), extend our knowledge to extra-sensory data; but we must feel and interpret through our inherent structure. Accident may rob us of part of our perceptual knowledge, individuals may differ in the keenness of their sensory discrimination, or in their degree of muscular strength or control; but the basic limits are, at a given period in the life of a species, set by inherited constitution.

It is notable in the history of biology that we most readily grasp the limitations and abilities of species which most closely resemble our own, in particular the mammalia. Where such endowments are in some way superior to our own they have been pressed into service to extend our powers, just as have tools and machinery. The horse is stronger than man, the dog has a keener sense of smell, both have been domesticated for thousands of years. Attributes further from our own, or less obviously useful, have by contrast only been understood in the light of patient scientific research. Only a knowledge of the principles by which sensory reactions work, and a comparable knowledge of the physical properties of the world beyond our immediate sensory information, has enabled us, for example, to understand the "language" of bees or the "hearing" of fishes. In science we go beyond the range of our direct experience to understand through an abstract, rather than a sensory knowledge, the world of other animals and the limitations of our own perceptual equipment. There is sufficient evidence that, while in many ways living creatures make use of the capacities of other species as we use the dog or the horse, man alone extends his world through abstract intellectual endeavour. This is one of the outstanding characteristics of man as a species. It is a process in which language is an essential component and which presupposes an immense capacity for learning, often of a highly abstract type; these are as much a feature of our human nature as the number of eyes, ears, arms and legs we have, or the type of digestive system.

In Chapter III I hope to say something about the way in which individuals differ in their heredity, but such a discussion loses much of its point if we forget in how much we are essentially alike, and how much more of our heredity goes to make us the same rather than different. Of course, people do differ from one another: they differ in eye, hair and skin colour, they differ in hair type, in height, in facial features and some minor anatomical structures. Even at their most extreme these variations are small compared with, for example, the variations which selective breeding has produced in dogs; we are very obviously one species. Because of our keen interest in the observable differences and the considerable social importance we attach to them, they seem great; but they are biologically minimal even at the physical level. The likeness extends beyond physical structure to psychological and behavioural characteristics; it is with this latter common inheritance that we are particularly concerned in this book.

## The organization of processes

In any consideration of the psychological and behavioural predispositions of the human race it is important to avoid sterile controversy about what is inherited and what is acquired. The approach in psychology which made the Nature-Nurture controversy seem real has been virtually exhausted. As so often happens with such arguments, it is finally agreed that there can be no answer to a question, which once looked quite reasonable, because it is the wrong question. In its simplest form the Nature-Nurture question was asked of such processes as walking in the form: "Do we learn to walk, or is it innate—something we just do?" The only possible answer is neither. The question is inappropriate, since it becomes apparent that we are built so that we can learn to walk, just as we are built so that we can learn to see. To argue the question in an either/or form makes no sense. A better question can now be phrased in terms of the amount and kind of learning necessary for particular behaviour patterns. Some things are much more clearly built in than others, so that the learning required to accomplish them is relatively slight, or in the normal course of events very likely to take place, though still necessary and perhaps effortful.

The conclusion to which we come, if we take this general view as a starting point, is that we observe a sort of sliding scale which follows a pattern that can be described in terms of relative invariance. A general outline may make the rest of the argument easier to follow. It can be stated with certainty that the number of precisely defined behaviour patterns which are inborn in man is small; they consist of a few reflex responses in the new-born infant, other reflexes involved in sexual intercourse and some social responses like smiling in babies; then there are a number of muscular and motor capacities which require some learning and practice, but vary very little in their learnt form, like chewing, walking and running. Finally there is a much larger area which can best be described as dispositions to learn in certain directions; these account for our learning to talk and to make many fine skilled movements, particularly those which depend on the co-ordination of hand and eye.

We can say that certain processes are latent in the organism —they require experience to become organized or manifest, but when this is given the pattern of the process can be predicted in advance. This is not quite the same as the process usually called maturation,[1] but akin to it. It means that though depth perception, and the perception of form, may take quite a long while to develop in the human infant, when they do manifest themselves they will obey certain well-known laws. They are learnt in one sense, but learnt to a pattern which is dictated by the character of the organism. At another level there is some evidence that social responsiveness is latent in this sense. Gross deformities and traumatic experiences may delay or inhibit the appearance of such undeveloped possibilities, but given a minimally normal set of organs and experiences they will function to a pattern. The importance of the principle is enormous—although its full limits have not yet been explored; it may hold for some of the intricate processes of thinking, imagination and feeling, but here the practical difficulties of adequate experiment are obvious and progress necessarily slow. Observation of, and experiment with, animals suggest the broad lines of the principle, and evidence for it is ample in the human field for the less subtle functions.

### Maturing to a pattern

The concept of instinct has been used to account for some aspects of man's behavioural heritage and may provide theories

[1] Maturation refers to something which appears late in the life of the organism but as a direct result of the growth processes that control the ordinary development of the person or animal—like growing teeth or reaching sexual maturity.

about the source and purpose of some of his activities, and further tell us something about the unlearnt stimuli for some unlearnt patterns of behaviour. In man and the higher animals it can be used in a loose way to describe predispositions to learn certain types of response, or to get satisfaction from achieving certain things which may depend largely on learning for their accomplishment. Since here it adds very little, and may even be misleading, it is probably better on the whole not to use it in this way. There are, however, certain groups of activities with which partly inherent dispositions are concerned, what we might call physiological maintenance (food, sleep, etc.), sexual and parental behaviour, the search for safety —the classification is at best a rough one. Nevertheless, much of what we learn and do is canalized to these ends: they are broad behavioural determinants. I propose to leave to the end of the chapter the problem of how best to describe these and to explore first the much more important idea that a predisposition for learning very complex behaviour exists in man. It is not helpful to call such a process instinctive; it is a realization of latent possibilities of which the patterning is predictable but the content is variable. It will be best understood through an example.

## Learning to talk

The learning of language is something so freely observable all around us as to pass almost unnoticed. We expect children to "learn" to talk, although we are aware that they learn to do so because the language that they talk will depend on the language that they hear, and if they do not hear any language then they do not talk. But unless the human child were so constructed that this everyday miracle could happen, such learning would never take place at all. This is a very simple thing to demonstrate. Children learn to talk in two ways, on the one hand from hearing other people talk and on the other from practising and imitating noises as their capacity to make the basic sounds that make up language matures, in the first year of life.

You can expose a chimpanzee[2] or a dog to precisely the same conditions as the child and it does not talk, partly because it cannot imitate the sounds, and partly because it does not have the right mental equipment. A dog will learn two sorts of language: its own, which is an emotive language which directly expresses and conveys its feelings, and a passive language in which it comes to recognize certain words as signals or signs for certain activities—dogs vary in how many of these they can acquire. A chimpanzee will usually get a wider range of this passive signal language than a dog and may even occasionally produce a word or two itself, but that is the limit. Many birds, on the other hand, have a much greater capacity for imitating sound and learning patterns of sound. Some species of bird have unlearnt calls which are expressive of feeling states and usually limited in range, others learn their songs from their parents and, reared by a different species, learn the songs and calls of the foster parents;[3] yet others have extremely developed powers of mimicry and can learn not only the calls of other birds and animals but quite sizeable human vocabularies, the familiar parrot and mina bird being good examples of the latter. Occasionally domesticated birds seem to use such language to what might be called good social effect, suggesting some level of "understanding", although in the main this seems confined to social and emotional interchange rather than the exchange of information; for example, the parrot may swear at the bishop just when you hoped it would not, and even appear pleased with the result, but is unlikely to give you a minute description of the burglar who stole your teaspoons.

By contrast, human language has a much wider range of

[2] Kellog, W. N. and Kellog, L. A., *The Ape and the Child*, McGraw-Hill, New York (1933).
[3] Thorpe, W. H., *Learning and Instinct in Animals*, page 400, Methuen, London (1963).

uses; even a small child will use language to express needs and emotions, as well as for social effect and to convey information and ask questions. To date there is no evidence that any other species can use language in this extremely flexible, original and creative way. Granted we have to learn to talk, once learnt, language becomes the basic tool of every aspect of living. In recent years the study of linguistics has revealed great structural variations in languages, and we have in this way become sensitive to differences which we once ignored. Exciting as much of this work has been, revealing possibilities of misunderstanding and confusion in the differences in the patterns of thought that are inherent in language,[4] it would be a pity if we allowed the existence of such interesting differences to obscure the much more obvious truth that any human language is, subtleties aside, roughly translatable into any other. When one comes to think of it this is something exceedingly remarkable because so much of language is completely abstract; that is, it has nothing to do with direct emotional expression, it is non-representative (the noises of the words are only rarely like the sound of the thing represented), it involves the manipulation of concepts about the world and experience which are reflective of human experience in the world. All this we take for granted; when someone speaks to us in a language we do not understand we assume, unless unusually insular, that it would express intelligible thoughts and information if we could only interpret it. This suggests that we enjoy certain common characteristics, ways of thinking and behaving, which are "human" however much they are learnt. People are such that they make up poetry, although they have to learn to do it. In the same way we tell stories of events or imagined events, communicate information and experience as well as share emotions, because we are that kind of creature.

I have gone into this in some detail because it serves to show how careful we must be in considering the whole ques-

[4] Lea Whorf, B., *Language, Thought and Reality*, Wiley, New York (1956).

tion of the "innate". It is naïve in the extreme to suppose that we can arrive at any proper idea of the nature of man by looking only for the so-called unlearnt patterns of behaviour and, because these are so few, saying, as some anthropologists did in their giddy heyday, that human nature is "infinitely malleable"; what they forgot was the basic likeness between people which enables us to understand and wonder at the differences among us. One has always to bear in mind that the victims of the inquiring psychologist or anthropologist are probably joined with them in a mutual wonder at each other's peculiarities; and this wonder they share because they are both human.

While we must look at these much broader principles to understand how potentiality becomes actuality in man, there are some more fixed patterns which may shape the direction in which the experience of the child is gained. When we consider these more specific patterns we can see that they too dictate very little but indicate a great deal; they confront the growing individual with the experiences which are our common human lot whatever we do with them, they provide the similarities which make the differences intelligible.

## THE UNLEARNED RESPONSE

### Ethology and man

Although in man the completely unlearned pattern of behaviour may be very rare, some of the most recent work on instinct in animals has a relevance to human behaviour that we should not overlook. These studies have been concerned with the specifics of the instinctual response. This is probably the only type of study in which the term has much real value any more and we owe our knowledge of it largely to the ethologist[5] who, following earlier leads given by the study of

---

[5] Such men as Armstrong, Lorenz, Thorpe and Tinbergen as well as many others; they are mainly zoologists by training rather than psychologists.

trophistic responses and chain reactions in lower organisms, examined the behaviour of birds and mammals in an attempt to get beyond the global idea of instinct as an explanation for animal behaviour. From these studies it has become apparent that such behaviour has two aspects, a configuration of stimuli (known as an *Innate Releasing Mechanism*, or IRM for short) in the animal's perceptual world, which calls forth the other aspect, a response which is highly predictable, the elements of which show very limited variation (known as a *Specific Action Pattern*, or SAP for short). Both the releaser and the action pattern can be analysed very minutely; they are few in number and sometimes involve curiously short-term learning processes which have been called *imprinting*. A typical example would be the sight of "eggs in a nest" as an IRM for brooding as a SAP. The just sufficient IRM here involves the total configuration of objects in a framework which must be within certain size limits, the "eggs" must be of a shape which approximates to round, the colour or marking of the eggs may or may not be important. It is possible that the natural stimulus may be somewhat less effective than what has been called a *super normal stimulus*; that is, the releaser has characteristics which are appropriate, but the match of the IRM to the stimulus is approximate rather than exact. When you have analysed all the components of a releaser (changing each item in turn to estimate its importance), it is usual to find that a certain number must be present but that they act in a cumulative way; any combination of the components may act as a releaser, the total number involved being more important than the presence of any particular one.

This is also true for the response pattern. Some people have argued that all that is needed to account for behaviour such as nest building are adequate IRMs and SAPs, but Thorpe,[6] at least, suggests that for the process to be effective there must be some idea of consummation or goal to be achieved, however dim that is; and his view seems the more convincing of

[6] *Op. cit.*, particularly pages 39 ff.

the two. Fuller accounts of these studies can be readily found elsewhere;[7] the methods by which the information is gained are fascinating in themselves and a remarkable tribute to the insight, imagination and persistence of the investigators. They have given us a key to a whole range of natural phenomena which we previously either marvelled at when it was successful, or laughed at when it failed. The contribution which such studies have made to an understanding of human behaviour is, although limited, significant. Among the simplest and most obviously inborn of such predictable responses to unlearnt stimuli many are usually described as producing emotion. The sudden loss of support will make a baby cry, so will a loud and unexpected noise, we identify both these reactions as expressions of fear. Other examples of inborn responses are less general than this; they appear to be rather simple reflexes (not that any reflex is really simple), the baby will turn its head if its cheek is touched and will suck objects introduced into its mouth, these two reflexes are the basis on which feeding is "learnt", a strong suckling response usually demands some little practice. Perhaps the best documented example of a response which involves a complex visual stimulus is the smiling response which Spitz[8] explored; this seems to follow more closely than the ones just mentioned the pattern of IRM and SAP which has become familiar in the animal studies.

## Smiling response

Round about three months a baby shown a moving mask, which needs to have only roughly these characteristics and be moving in the direction indicated, will make the baby smile—any old face similarly nodding has the same effect. Here we have both the

[7] Among those that are both easy to read and easy to obtain, there are, for example, Lack, *The Life of the Robin*, Withersby, London (1943); and Lorenz, K., *King Solomon's Ring*, Methuen, London (1952).

[8] Spitz, R., "The Smiling Response", *Genet. Psychol. Monogr.* (1946), **34**, 57–125.

*innate releasing mechanism* and the *specific action pattern* which are together concerned both with the communication and expression of emotion. The stage is fleeting; by the time it is six months old the baby is considerably more interested in whose face it is that smiles than the mere expression, and it will often cry when it sees a mask or a strange face, however benevolent. This is trying for its parents; at one minute they seem to have a nice friendly baby who smiles at everyone, the next he suddenly turns into a fussy individual likely to smile at the milkman and scream at his grandmother. All this really means is that his social responses have passed from the reflex stage into a socially meaningful one and, even if his social behaviour is not now what everyone wants, it is undeniably his own.

Lorenz has suggested a few more of these *innate releasers* in human beings, which are worth noting although the evidence for them is much less compelling. Anything with roughly the head shape and proportions of a baby is said to elicit mothering behaviour in the adult, for example, dogs with rounded heads rather than pointed ones; the argument is tenuous, but if one looks at what has happened to domesticated lap dogs, it is suggestive at any rate. Many baby animals are this sort of shape and they are usually found attractive, so that the argument is obviously not entirely spurious.

## The following response

A more complex and important example which involves the idea of *imprinting* has been discussed by Bowlby.[9] He feels that the baby's capacity for human feeling depends on the attachment to the mother, which is acquired to a pattern, one which involves principles derived from the study of animals. Briefly, *imprinting* is the name which has been given to a form of short-term learning in the immature organism; the animal is

[9] Bowlby, J., "Symposium on 'Psycho-analysis and Ethology' II: Ethology and the Development of Object Relation", *Inter. J. of Psych. Anal.* (1960), **41**, 313.

born with a readiness to learn in some direction, more particularly to show a particular pattern of response to an object which has a few broadly defined characteristics. Once a real object having these characteristics has been responded to it becomes "fixed", in its particularity, as an object of the response. For example, a baby chicken emerging from its egg will in natural circumstances first see the hen, and will "learn" to respond to her by following her; once this has happened it will show great distress when separated from her. In the absence of a hen it will become attached, in the same way, to anything which is roughly the right size and which moves, even to a flickering light or a moving disc.[10] Once established, the imprinted object will be followed by the chick rather than some more biologically appropriate object. Although, when it was first demonstrated, this process was held to be irreversible, some doubt has now been thrown on this; there is some evidence that a stimulus which has more of the "right" characteristics may be preferred to the imprinted object if introduced early enough.

In general it can be said that such imprinted releasers are hard to change, and that a critical or sensitive learning period exists in which they are readily fixed; thereafter they continue to elicit appropriate behaviour. There is also considerable evidence that, since imprinting the mother automatically sets up a pattern of "following", there is typical distress when the young animal is separated from her. Finally, this process of imprinting apparently plays an important part in establishing species identification, even of suitable sexual objects later in life; put anthropomorphically, the young animal "thinks of itself" as a member of the same species as the rearing animal.

According to Bowlby the baby learns its mother's face in the first two to four months of life. Once learnt (or imprinted) this comes to have a specialized capacity to allay fear responses,

[10] Smith, F. V. and Hoyes, P. A., "Properties of the visual stimuli for Approach Response in the domestic chick", *Animal Behaviour* (1961), **9**, 159–66.

or to create them if it disappears for a long time. It thus becomes a predetermined but learnt refuge in grief.[11] Babies demonstrably become attached to their mothers in a forceful fashion, separation obviously causes them distress. So long as the attachment to the mother is explained in terms of her learned value as a food supply, it is difficult in the early months to see why food alone fails to satisfy, even more puzzling to explain the attachment of children to clearly "bad" mothers. If, on the other hand, the child learns to respond to the mother directly, through a process of imprinting, then one can see that her disappearance causes a direct sense of loss which has nothing to do with food and much to do with the arousal of an unlearnt fear response.

In societies where, unlike our own, babies are handed round a lot and breast-fed by a variety of people it seems likely that this response is more generalized; the fear response probably arises only when the baby is separated from people and its fears will be allayed by people in general, provided they have roughly the right appearance (that is, a baby used to brown people might, and usually in fact does, find white people frightening) but this is getting more speculative.

As the child grows older it depends less and less on its mother and the "following" response system begins to wear off; the child finds other and more general ways of coping with fear and keeping anxiety under control.

If any further evidence is needed that the mother calls forth a following response, then we have only to watch a baby at the toddling stage pursue its mother relentlessly round the house. A secure baby will make do with other people for quite long periods unless something upsets it; but pain, fear or unfamiliar surroundings will produce demands, vocal or otherwise, for its mother. A child of two or so in a play group which is new to it will go in pursuit of its mother every few minutes (if she is available) and then back to the toys and other children; as the situation becomes more familiar the intervals will

[11] *Op. cit.*

increase up to two or three hours at a time. Clearly, children will stand longer separations than this without trauma; all this indicates is what the child will voluntarily do if the choice is his.

The importance of the mother's face in this assuagement of fear can be seen by leaving a child in a strange room with its mother on a chair in the middle; it will begin to explore away from the mother but its furthest forays will be in front of her rather than behind; so that the child's movements will describe an oval of increasing size keeping close to the mother's back and further ranging from her face.[12] Children differ a good deal

in the strength and persistence of this following response, probably because of differences, either innate or acquired, in their sensitivity to anxiety; but this is the general pattern.

*Learning the unlearnt response*

It seems, then, that although we have relatively few unlearnt responses compared with the lower animals, they are important in infancy, in establishing the first human attachments. We share many of our needs with other animals but have a greater degree of flexibility in satisfying them. Whatever the equipment with which we come into the world, even in our earliest months learning of some kind is critical even to the emergence of patterns of behaviour which are themselves more or less reflex in character. Both for the primates and man very little complex adult behaviour can be accounted for in terms of innate disposition; experience and learning themselves determine the manifest form of the latent innate response. A recent scientific

[12] Arsenian, J. M. reported in Baldwin, A. L., *Psychological Development* (1952), University of Kansas, pp. 168–9 in the duplicated text.

horror story makes it clear that one cannot separate instinct from learning; that the two are bound together in an exceedingly complex way. The story of Harlow's[13] experiments with rhesus monkeys is sufficiently important to be worth describing at least briefly, since I think it has a critical importance for our understanding of this dependence of the predictable future on the apparently remote past. Also these experiments are among some of the most brilliant that have been done in recent years.

Harlow tried to find the elements in a monkey "mother" which made it adequate and satisfactory to the baby. He made a notable discovery when he found that a substitute model foster mother was vastly preferred by the monkey when it was soft[14] even if he had to take his food from another less acceptable model. Further, when parted from his wooden faced, terry-towelling-covered "mother", the young monkey showed acute distress; when she was present he clung to her in any strange places, and generally behaved as if she was his stronghold in a hard and lonely world. This study has considerable importance of its own and led Bowlby to the conclusions I have suggested above; but all was not as well as it seemed. When Harlow[15] followed up the monkeys so reared in adult life, he found that when they mixed with others similarly reared later they appeared to get on fairly well with them; but they never displayed any adult sexual behaviour either to each other or to more normally reared monkeys. This suggested that, though sexual activity might in the direct sense be unlearnt, it quite obviously depended on earlier experience of physical contact with a live animal or person in order to occur. He eventually got a few of the females to mate with normal males and, when in due course they had babies, they seemed

---

[13] Harlow, H. F., "The Nature of Love", *Amer. Psychologist* (1958), **13**, 673–85.

[14] The "soft" model consisted of a wire frame covered with foam rubber and terry towelling—the other model was an uncovered wire frame. Both had wooden heads with "faces".

[15] Harlow, H. F., "The Heterosexual Affectional System in Monkeys", *American Psychologist* (1962), **17**, p. 8, 1.

to have absolutely no idea what to do with them, simply ignored them or trod on them. Now normally reared monkeys cope quite adequately with the new experience of motherhood in the ordinary course of events. They have not learnt it, in the sense that no one tells them how to do it, but evidently their own experience of mothering is critical to their capacity for it. These experiments enable us to see something of the way unlearnt drive may interact with critical learning experience to produce a later apparently unrelated response. They show that in our nearest animal relations early social experience is more important than hormones, even in areas of behaviour which we think of as essentially depending on unlearnt instinctual drives.

## EMOTION

### Emotion as an inborn character

In much of the preceding section which dealt with unlearned responses it was necessary to talk of emotions; many innate releasing mechanisms produce "fear" or "following" and it seems appropriate now to consider the way in which emotion may be best understood as part of our heredity. The emotions are usually said to develop; we believe that we can identify them in ourselves and others; certainly they are of critical importance in psychology as they are in life.

It has been argued [16] that emotions mobilize and organize us rather than needs, drives or instincts. Such a view has the merit that it avoids many of the theoretical difficulties of the drive theories that will be discussed in the next section. Whatever the advantages or disadvantages of such a theory, it is certain that the vast majority of authors from Freud and McDougal onwards have given a central importance to the emotions, and argued that at least emotion is intimately associated with drive even when they still find this latter notion indispensable.

[16] For a complete account of such a view see Arnold, M. *Emotion and Personality,* Cassell, London (1960).

The majority of psychologists agree that patterns of emotional response are, in ways I have already suggested, primitive and unlearnt aspects of human nature. Even Watson,[17] in the extremity of his denial of the importance of the innate compared with the learnt, suggested that fear, rage and love were unlearnt responses. Perhaps typically, the dimmer emotions have received most attention and psychologists have less to say about joy and happiness than about anger and fear.

## Recognizing emotions

First of all it may be useful to consider the problem of recognizing emotions, since if we are going to talk about it we need to assume we can identify it; this is more difficult than it might seem at first sight. Darwin[18] tried to explore the problem of emotional expression, others have followed; the degree of success attending all has been small. In the earlier part of this century psychologists everywhere showed people pictures of actresses expressing a large variety of emotions which people were rather unsuccessful in identifying, but nothing like as unsuccessful as later judges were with unposed photographs of people just experiencing emotion. Films of babies "emoting" were notorious, since no one was any use at deciding what was wrong at all (there was always something wrong—people can, it has been found, tell the difference between a smile and a bellow).[19] From this evidence some people have drawn the inference that there are no expressions

[17] Watson in his *Behaviour: an Introduction to Comparative Psychology,* published in 1914, put forward the then revolutionary and explosive view that everything we were apart from a few simple reflexes and emotions was learnt. He further held that only behaviour was worth studying, that we could gain no knowledge worth having from reported experience or introspection. He had an enormous, and in the main healthy, influence on the subsequent history of psychology.

[18] Darwin, C., *The Expression of Emotion in Man and Animals.*

[19] Cf. Sherman, H., 1927, "The differentiation of emotional responses in infants: II. The ability of the observer to judge the emotional characteristics of the crying of infants, and of the voice of an adult", *J. Comp. Psychol.,* **7**, 335–51.

characteristic of particular emotions, and others that emotions are undifferentiated. But other possibilities suggest themselves. The fact that people are more successful in identifying posed "emotions" than "real" ones could be accounted for by suggesting that within any culture there are certain conventions for expressing emotions and these we learn in a large measure, gross differences perhaps apart; there is a good deal of subsidiary evidence to support this point of view. The "real" emotions are a problem partly because they are nearly always mixed and may be inaccurately reported. To give a crude example, if you make someone do something unpleasant in order to get a photograph of "disgust" he may well be both attracted and repelled, even if it is a situation in which conventionally he ought to be disgusted; if he is all that disgusted he will refuse to do it anyway without more coercion than can be exercised in a laboratory using volunteer subjects.

The only state of emotional arousal which we seem to be able to describe with accuracy and recognize with ease is the "startle" pattern, which seems to be quite genuinely unlearnt and even reflex in nature, but even here the stimuli differ for different people once infancy is passed. The other thing that the failure to recognize pictures of emotions suggests is that we normally identify these largely by context, movement, sound and so on. Even when the person says nothing to explain himself, if he is running away from a bull, white in the face, sweating and making a sobbing cry, we shall not be far wrong if we identify his behaviour as expressing fear, even if his bared teeth might suggest anger or effort in a different context. This is true even of animals identifying emotions in other animals; apart from a few innate releasers, they need some context as well. But we find that our normal identification of emotion from facial expression, however inaccurate, is considerably better than our capacity to identify it in monkeys and vice versa. You have to know a good deal about apes and monkeys to get your identification right, but once you have done so it is quite possible; it can, in a word, be learnt. Yet some responses even here are easier to identify than others and the context may need to give us minimal clues. We think up simple clue systems, dogs wag their tails when pleased, cats do so when angry etc., and become rather cross when this does not entirely work and the dog bites us while wagging his tail.

## Development in emotional response

It is well to bear in mind the difficulty of identifying an emotion just by the look on someone's face, or even the noise he is making, when we come to consider work on the development of emotions. The fashionable point of view is that the newborn infant in fact is capable of only two emotional states, rest and undifferentiated excitement. Although this is the orthodox belief, a certain cynicism may not be out of place, since the undifferentiated state could conceivably be in the eye of the beholder; a baby's capacity for self-expression is pretty limited physically. It is suggested that other emotions become distinguishable during the first and second years of life, so that the baby comes to experience and express fear, anger, joy, love and so forth as recognizable emotions. Whatever view one takes of the baby's initial emotional capacity, it seems clear that part of the way in which emotion is expressed is unlearnt, and part of it learnt, or at least acquired in the process of growth; both tears and laughter are absent in the newborn child, but nearly everyone acquires the capacity for both in the first year of life, however little they may use it later. Clearly, language makes it much easier to be sure about the differences, especially when emotion is complex; I would go so far as to say that without language many of the finer shades of emotional experience would be impossible.

Emotions, however they start, palpably acquire considerable distinctness. We can broadly classify emotions in their grosser forms but as we really experience them in the shades and mixtures that give meaning and colour to life they are very hard to define. Blinding rage may be easily recognized while a faint nostalgia is neither so easily seen nor so readily classified, although it may on balance be a more common emotion. Only the very broad outlines of the emotional map are clearly pre-determined, we refine and emphasize this in terms of our experience, and the conditions of our life will determine with which emotions we are most familiar. Yet even the less crude emotions can be discovered and understood so readily that they are clearly part of the probable human experience into which we grow. Some give pleasure, others pain,[20] all seem to move us to action in some degree, and this is why it is dangerous to think of emotion as essentially disrupting, however true this may be of some strongly realized emotional reactions. A narrow view of emotion dealing only with paralysing fear, blinding rage, unbearable joy, may give some substance to the view that emotion disrupts, since we note them especially as inter-fering with our ability to cope with life; but this is rather like arguing that because a flood can be a disaster, water is essen-tially dangerous rather than useful.

## The organization of emotions

It has already been argued that emotion plays a strong part in the determination of behaviour; emotions are aroused within the framework of a need pattern and interact with it to create a pattern of purpose in the individual. This pattern of purpose is partly cognitive, that is, it has meaning realized in some intellectual process however crude. The elaborate capacity for abstract thinking and long-term memory characteristic of people allow persistent states of partial mobilization of emotion around objects, situations and ideas, which we can perhaps best describe as sentiments or enduring emotional attitudes. Such emotional dispositions are self-maintaining to the extent that the presence of a situation, person or object is no longer necessary for it to act as a powerful stimulus to behaviour which is emotionally related to it.

Emotions aroused in one situation may be discharged in another; at its simplest this means that events may create an

[20] Cf. Chapter V.

emotional mood which carries over into situations beyond them. There are more complicated effects than this, some of which can best be described as general emotional dispositions, others as deflections or ego-defence mechanisms and yet others as "displacement". Of these, the last is something that we readily see in animals and can describe fairly well. As ethologists like Lorenz[21] describe the process, it may involve rather elaborate theoretical models, but all we really need to say is that when an animal is in a general state of arousal (a state which can be called a drive state but which has a distinct emotional quality), together with some conflict about its appropriate expression in behaviour, then the energy so mobilized tends to be discharged in an irrelevant and inappropriate manner. It is common for this discharge to become somewhat ritualized or at any rate typical; thus a cat roused to agitation or fear may well start "washing" if it cannot escape, or a hunted animal may sometimes kill prey it cannot eat, apparently as an over-flow of aroused fear too great to be fully used in escape. Such displacement is a response to frustration in some form and in time may come to replace more or less permanently part of the appropriate behaviour. In human psychology the term is still useful, either to account for behaviour following frustration or more simply as discharge of an energy mobilized in excess of the requirements of the situation.

It is this over-arousal which has, I think, given rise to some commonly held, though rather obviously erroneous, ideas about the nature of emotion. We are inclined to think of emotion as typically disturbing rather than facilitating because when it is adequate to the activity in hand we notice the activity more than the emotion; only when it cannot be used to meet the demands of the immediate situation are we aware of it just as emotion. I have not perhaps made it clear that in spite of

[21] Lorenz, K., "The comparative method in studying innate behaviour", page 221. In Danielli (ed.) *Physiological Mechanisms in Animal Behaviour, S.E.B. Symposium No. 4.* Cambridge University Press, Cambridge (1950).

the possibility of persistence in an emotion once aroused and never discharged, emotions are essentially phenomena of reaction. That is, emotions do not exist *sui generis* awaiting an opportunity to display themselves, they are called forth by experience; individuals differ in how sensitive they are to emotion-provoking stimuli, but not in the quantity of emotion they start with. The issue is somewhat obscured by the way in which emotion once aroused may remain undischarged and hence colour future action; in one way or another they may become cumulatively motivating. If we say someone is bad-tempered we may either mean that it takes very little to make him angry or that anger colours all his attitudes; this is not at all the same thing.

We are most familiar with the idea of control of aroused emotion which finds no obvious immediate use in action in the theory of the ego-defence mechanisms. These are ideas which are much more complex than that contained in the idea of displacement activity, since they are usually presented as part of a theory of personality. In this context we can best describe them by saying that emotions which threaten the organization of the self, or which go beyond what action is felt to be possible in the situation, are in some way excluded from the conscious awareness of the person. They may be repressed or denied, or they may be projected on to other people so that what starts as a personal feeling is perceived as coming from outside. Whether such emotions are projected or repressed they tend to endure either because they are discharged in only a limited way, or because they become the typical mode of emotional expression. These processes, because they are by definition excluded from consciousness, tend to be crude and to have a very restricted logic of their own, often a logic typical of the stage of intellectual development at which the mechanism first came into play.

Finally, there is the persistent emotional mood of the individual. This may depend in part on genetically determined levels of sensitivity to different emotions, and in part on the quality of emotion to which the person has been exposed in the past, which has been aroused in him. Expectations are thus established which colour present experience and in time trigger off responses with minimal stimuli; the person in whom the pervasive emotional mood is fear needs little to frighten him, the secure and happy person will be much less ready to see a threat. The chronically hostile will be ever ready to look for an insult which would be non-existent to a more friendly person. Much human motivation can best be understood in terms of such enduring patterns of emotional organization, just because they have this self-reinforcing quality.

## Emotional maturity

If we say that it is emotion which gives colour to life, which moves us to action, which helps to define our purposes and values, then it is clear that emotional control, or emotional maturity, cannot be a state in which one has no emotions, but rather in which the emotions do not disrupt and destroy. It is necessary to say this because people talk and behave as if the ideal human state was one in which emotion played no part. Really you might just as well be dead. Confronting the enraged three-year-old, biting and screaming mad, it might occur to you that what you needed to cultivate in him was a state in which anger could not, and did not, occur—this is in fact not as difficult as it sounds, but the penalty is extreme. He needs to learn to cope with and use his anger, not to forgo it. If he continues to express it in his characteristic three-year-old way he will be a social menace when he is grown up. If he gives up being angry, he will be a colourless nonentity and probably have ulcers. If he learns to tolerate frustration and to use his anger to overcome difficulties and to work off the surplus in digging the garden or writing pamphlets, he will be a reasonable human being. Without a capacity for anger he may lack a capacity for compassion and for the vigorous action which the frustrations of life may demand. Without the capacity to mobilize energy to combat difficulty, the world would be a jungle; without the capacity to control and contain anger we may well make it a desert.

In the same way we may think that the love of a baby is egotistical and demanding, as hard to bear at times as his anger, but if he never learns to value others or learns merely to be solidly indifferent, then he will have nothing to give, or no impulse to give in human relations.

Control and balance are what characterize emotional maturity, not total detachment. It is not for nothing that we speak of people as being moved to anger, or love or compassion; or that we value in people such capacity for a response which is something more than a logical appraisal of the situation in which they find themselves. We know only too well that charity without love is cold, that it injures while it remedies. On the other hand, we think of people whose actions are governed by emotions as unreliable, often illogical and frequently dangerous. Such emotional lability consists usually in responding always to the stimulus and mood of the moment; in this sense some people are clearly more emotional than others, and it is their degree of manifest disturbance rather than their effectiveness which catches our attention. Such immediacy of response often lacks the coherence that is characteristic of emotional maturity, where the structuring of emotion into sentiments and values gives a long-term pattern and stability to the whole personality. This is something to which I shall return in a later chapter since it demands more detailed discussion. Perhaps it is worth adding that the congruence of thought and feeling which characterizes emotional maturity makes any attempt to think of emotion as something that opposes "reason" untenable as a general principle; they can come apart but they do not belong apart.

## SOURCES OF ENERGY

### The Why of Behaviour

The discussion of the patterning of behaviour and of experience through broadly inherent or latent processes which I

have attempted in the preceding section has deliberately omitted
what is often called the motivation problem. The *why* rather
than the *how* of human behaviour. This has been done partly
because this motivation problem, which has loomed so large
in psychology, may take our attention away from things which
we really know something about, and partly because there is
more than a suspicion that *the* motivation problem is spurious.
For the same reason I avoided a discussion of instinct until
this point; it has so often been used as if it were explanatory
that it is apt to blind us to processes which are more critical
to an adequate psychology.

In this section I have attempted to outline some of the
major and conflicting theories of motivation and to comment
on their strengths and weaknesses. Even if the motivation problem turns out in the end to be all about nothing, it has been
too important in psychology to be quietly ignored. Theories
proliferate here and none of them seems sufficiently good to
oust the others from the field; but we can see some general
conclusions which indicate the lines along which this problem
may be best understood.

Probably the strongest contrast to a theory of instinct is
provided by those who hold that it is unnecessary to postulate
any energy source in the organism, still less to label it in this
way; since organisms when alive have energy as a datum, all
one needs to talk about is what determines the direction in
which they use it. Such a theory has been advanced by people
with widely different views; Skinner[22] in his operant conditioning theory, in which he suggests that motivation questions
are futile in psychology, makes use of it, and so in a totally
different way does Leeper[23] in advancing the view that emotions
motivate rather than needs, drives or instincts. For these people
the questions about why people do what they do will be very

[22] Skinner, *Cumulative Record*, Appleton-Century-Crofts, New York
(1959), pages 202 ff. especially.
[23] Leeper, R. W., "A Motivational Theory of Emotion", *Psychol. Rev.*
(1948), **55**, 5.

specific, while for those who hold an instinct theory broad general questions will be more important.

## Instinct as energy

In colloquial speech "instinctive" is simply an equivalent of unreflecting automative response. This use of the term has little technical significance. The traditional philosophical use is more precise, being (roughly from Aristotle onwards) used to describe patterns of animal behaviour which achieved goals for the animal which it could not "know" or foresee; such behaviour was unlearnt and although "blind" highly effective in maintaining the life of the individual and the species. The term covered a wide range of behavioural possibilities and it was descriptive of a category of efficient but non-rational behaviour; it always carried with it as an undertone the notion of irresistible impulse, as does the more popular use.

The concept of instinct has been taken into psychology and developed in different ways of which three are notable: one concerns the impulse to behaviour, the source of energy; the second is descriptive of a class of behaviour, and the third concerned with the minutiae of the behaviour itself. From the first we derive the psychology of drive; from the second the idea of goal and need; and from the third a "stimulus", "response" psychology of the kind so successfully developed by the ethologists whose work has already been discussed.

The idea of instinct as a powerful force within the human organism impelling it to action receives its most explicit and important formation in psycho-analytic theory. In Freud's account of personality structure the source of action and drive within the individual, which he called the "id", is modified and restrained by other aspects of the personality which develop later in time and arise as a result of the individual's experience of the world around him. The notion that this force was sexual in a broad sense, blind and self-seeking, justified his use of the idea of instinct in this context. In later formulations he came to see two opposing instinctual drives, the life instinct and the death instinct. In this he moved away from the notion of a single energy source to a formulation which included the idea of different goals, or ends, to which energy was striving. The whole theory is exceedingly complex and this is only one aspect of it, but since it is the one which concerns us at the moment it is important to see that it has at least these two facets, the idea of energy source and the idea of goal. Much less explicitly, but as an important ancillary feature, there is the idea that particular patterns of action express the drive and constitute its goal at different phases of development— typically this runs the gamut from the sucking response in the baby to sexual intercourse in the adult, but attention is not given to the details of the patterns but to the broad psychological context in which they arise. Basically, Freud's theory of instinct is a general motivation theory, in which energy has one goal from which it may be, perhaps necessarily is, deflected, but which remains forever immutable in essence.[24]

Accompanying this motivation theory is a second principle of considerable importance: that the organism seeks, above all else, pleasure; this is not quite the goal of energy but its guiding principle. The most extreme expression of such psychological hedonism is to be found in early psychoanalytic theory, although many others accept it without question as an *a priori* postulate, a self-evident truth. The "Pleasure Principle" creates so many theoretical difficulties that its own mother would not know it by the time it has been squeezed and stretched to cover every human action. The apparently simple hedonism of the principle is weakened when it is suggested that altruistic behaviour satisfies the pleasure principle when it denies the person obvious pleasure, even life itself: thus the starving man who gives food to the starving child can be said to satisfy the pleasure principle in the sense that he maintains his self-regard although he denies his appetite for food. This is a very subtle,

[24] Jung propounded a very similar theory; though he made much less of the idea of instinct than Freud, he was equally convinced of the Unconscious as the source of striving psychic life in the individual.

though in its way valid, argument and one that is not always appreciated by those who are busy being shocked by the idea that we all go around determined to enjoy life. In fact it is much the same argument as St Thomas uses in suggesting that the "good" gives pleasure and is attractive for this reason. Both are a long way from the exaggerated puritanism of those who appear to favour the view that the unpleasant is always good and the pleasant necessarily bad, a negative print of the simple hedonistic argument and equally naïve.

## Descriptive systems

The classical example of a more purely descriptive use of the idea of instinct is that advanced by McDougal,[25] who proposed an extensive list of human propensities. His list ranged from food-seeking, mating and the like, to home-making and self-regard, and contained between ten and fifteen categories in his various reworkings of the idea. He used the word propensity, particularly in his later writing, to make a distinction between these broad inherent inclinations and the highly specific chain responses which people like Fabre and Lloyd Morgan had described in animals. McDougal's system does very little to enable us to understand human action; it merely codes the way people behave and suggests that, since they behave like this, then they have an impulse so to behave—a certain circularity of argument is inevitable. Valuable as such descriptive classification can be at a certain stage in scientific inquiry, it can never be more than a starting point for an explanation and hence doomed to obsolescence from the start.

## The need/drive theory

The only way in which descriptive motivation theories of this kind have been substantially developed is in what might be called a need/drive theory which, whatever its limitations, has been found sufficiently workable as a theory to become a standard feature of contemporary psychology. Once again it

[25] For example, *Energies of Men*, 8th ed. Methuen, London (1950).

eschews the more thorny aspects of the concept of instinct and substitutes in its place the idea that the organism is moved to action only when its equilibrium is disturbed by some deficiency within the system. The organism then acts to correct that deficiency and once again sinks into inertia. Such a concept has been used by psychologists of widely different schools, interests and approaches as a basic premise, and its respectability is enshrined for ever in nearly all contemporary textbooks. Part of the success of this idea has been its flexibility; calling certain drives primary and others secondary, and suggesting that all the secondary drives rest ultimately on the primary ones (being acquired by learning). Any piece of behaviour can theoretically be accounted for even if the theory cannot actually be demonstrated to hold good for any particular instance.

The theory in greater detail goes like this: the primary drives are those with an obvious physiological basis, mostly concerned with recurrent needs in the organism; thus there is a need for water, food, sleep, sexual satisfaction; to this a maternal drive is added in the case of the female, and that is virtually all. In the main this theory has been worked out with the white rat in mind, which gives it limitations, but in this case it is often assumed that the rat is a sort of model or prototype for the mammalia including man. These primary needs, with the exception of sexual behaviour, can be shown to be essential to life. The sexual need is essential to the maintenance of the species as is the maternal need. Other "needs" are acquired through processes which can broadly be described as learning, but are more often described as "conditioned", since the process whereby the person acquires them is said to be one in which the originally biologically adequate experience or stimulus is replaced by an originally absent or neutral one, or in which certain actions are carried out because in the end they satisfy a need which would not otherwise be satisfied. An example of the first sort of replacement would be a need to read or be entertained, of the second, working for money in order to buy food which you need in the straight-forward sense. Now it has been repeatedly demonstrated, from the time when Pavlov first contrived to make a dog salivate at the sound of a bell, that all sorts of bodily responses can be conditioned to occur in the face of originally neutral stimuli: large numbers of babies acquire a marked dislike for people in white coats after one of these has given them an injection, and so on. Similarly, it is patently obvious that in complex civilizations primary needs are satisfied in incredibly distant and complicated ways, some of which become satisfying in them-selves.

## Homeostasis and the problem of the passive organism

The system has, however, its weakness right at the centre. The so-called primary needs are real enough, but even for the rat they are not the whole story. The division of "primary" needs, with demonstrable physiological lack creating a drive to satisfaction, with all its convenience in terms of units of strength in degree of deprivation (hours without food, for example) or units of satisfaction (pellets of food consumed), does not cover all that the animal does without learning. The idea that the animal is inert and passive in a state of physio-logical satisfaction turns out to be false, as does the idea that it learns only when driven to by necessity of this kind. Most animals are curious, the more intelligent the more curious on the whole. They like wandering about and poking their noses into things; it even seems possible to say without stretching the imagination too far that many of them are capable of experi-encing boredom. So apparent has this become that the term "exploratory drive" has been coined to account for this as a further "primary" need. But while the evidence for such a need is overwhelming, only casuistry can equate it with the other primary needs as being a measurable physiological lack.

At this point the whole tidy system totters; it has been propped up in one way or another because it is such a useful idea, but the only logical conclusion that one can arrive at is that so admirably argued by Thorpe[26] that animals are organisms so built that they seek and organize experience by virtue of being alive, that they learn because they are built that way not because they are driven to it by direct biological lack. They seek experience partly for its own sake and in so doing they learn (whether one dresses this up and calls it "latent learning" or not is really beside the point). This sort of formulation accounts much more satisfactorily for why children learn to talk or skip or stand on their heads than any primary need idea. It also becomes obvious that much of the argument which led Freud, Watson and others to suggest that sociability was learnt rather than inherent falls by the wayside. Once one admits in principle that organisms seek satisfaction other than food, water, sleep, sex, etc., then there is no particular reason for excluding other needs from this primary category. It then becomes diabolically difficult to decide which are learnt needs and which inherent in the organism. But it is certainly obvious that the more complex the organism the greater the part played by what one might call more cognitive needs: a monkey, for example, will learn to operate a fairly complex mechanism which rewards it with a thirty-second view through a window of another room; it works harder at this if something is going on there. Animals kept in very limited, very dull environments from birth either lose much of this inherent curiosity or become "silly" in that they respond wildly and randomly to anything that attracts their wandering attention.[27] Animals and people deprived of all sensory stimulation experience apparently not merely boredom, but acute distress; they need constant sensory stimulation even to achieve what is usually regarded as homeostasis or a passive condition of satiation.

[26] Thorpe, W. H., *Learning and Instinct in Animals. Op. cit.*

[27] Hebb has suggested that the central nervous system is "stimulus hungry"; in the famous coffin experiments at McGill, where volunteers were deprived of as much sensation as possible, they very quickly became confused, hallucinated and generally disorganized both physiologically and psychologically.

## The concept of emergent hierarchy

From all of this, which may seem just a muddle of conflicting ideas, certain undisputed facts begin to emerge. Whatever we may do with the idea of instinct, we have to reckon
in animals and men with a set of satisfactions which it is typical
of them to seek. Whatever we may do with the notion of energy
source, it is apparent that we share with our animal relations
certain needs for air, food, water, sexual satisfaction, in certain
circumstances parental behaviour, an inherent curiosity about
the world around us and a set towards learning in the sense
of organizing our experience in a way which enables us to
draw upon it. It is highly probable and well argued, for example
by Harding,[28] that we need and seek the company of other
people for its own sake. A good deal of our behaviour can be
accounted for in these terms since these are among the universal
inherent characteristics of man. We may go further, like Maslow,[29] and argue that our needs are arranged in an emergent
hierarchy. This is different from saying that some are primary
and others derived from these, but argues rather that some are
more urgent than others, so that unless they are satisfied we
fail to recognize the presence of other and less pressing wants.
He suggests that physiological needs come first, then safety
needs, then love needs, then the need for self-esteem and finally
the need for self-actualization, which last includes aesthetic
and cognitive needs. The system suggests that such energy as
the organism has available will be expended on satisfying the
most pressing of these. He also suggests that once satisfaction
has been experienced, it may more easily later be forgone in
the face of a higher need. He further adds that only partial
satisfaction seems to be necessary before the next need begins
to be experienced; but he does suggest that few people get to
the point of what he calls self-actualization, where the lower

[28] Harding, D. W., *Social Psychology and Individual Values*, Hutchinson, London (1953).
[29] Maslow, *Motivation and Personality*, Harper, New York (1954).

needs are all subordinated to the person's becoming what "he must be".

Whatever we may do with the energy problem, it at least seems possible to conclude that it is sensible to talk of determinants of behaviour which are common to us all by virtue of our human nature. Many of these determinants exercise their influence more through the way in which our experience is patterned, than in its precise content, although the exact limits of such patterning are still uncertain. Finally, it seems that we have a number of predispositions to learn and behave in certain ways which vary considerably in the degree to which they are binding; most take the form of an inherent readiness to learn in some direction, but vary in how quick, inevitable and irreversible such learning must be.

# CHAPTER II

# MAN IN SOCIETY

## *WHAT THE CULTURE GIVES*

### *Membership of society*

It will, I hope, have become obvious by this time that the talk about a human being as a biological and psychological entity without reference to the culture in which he lives is more or less futile. Even his sensory acuity and his digestion will reflect that culture, and infinitely more so will his habits of thought and social behaviour, his interests and his skills reflect the world of people in which he has been reared. For most people the world into which they are born is that in which they are brought up—but the rare exceptions suggest that we are what we are brought up to be in a very large measure, that is to say, that a child reared in an English-speaking community with an advanced technology and a standard system of education will be a literate English-speaking individual with some understanding of mechanical devices. He will differ to some extent in temperament from other members of the community, he may be more skilled in some respects and less in others— more or less able to cope with the opportunities, difficulties and challenges of life. This is not particularly surprising— with a few noteworthy exceptions, in the way of gross physical deficiencies, the difference between cultures over-rides the differences in genetic endowments which we observe.

On the other hand, although the person is in so great a part made by his social and cultural environment, even this does not limit him in any final sense. Once the person has grown to psychological maturity, he can, given intelligence, opportunity and effort, acquire the language and habits of another, but the older he is the harder it will be for him to do so and the more of a top dressing his second culture will be, and the greater the difference the greater the difficulty. Many people forced into such situations find it too difficult, others actively resist acculturation. In the history of the world and in the world as we know it today, conquest, migration, forced movement of people is, and always has been, recognized as a source at once of sorrow and suffering and at the same time of change in ways of life, language, law, political structure and so forth. As far as recorded history goes back there has always been a refugee problem; the exile, whether he strives to adjust himself to his new life, or strives to retain his cultural identity against overwhelming odds, is always to some extent a sufferer and usually the older he is the greater his problems.

This may be very self-evident but it is perhaps useful in giving the emotional significance to the idea than an individual both lives in his culture and creates it while he lives within it.

## Basic personality[1]

I have suggested that age has something to do with how readily we can change our habits of mind and living, but even before speech establishes both the possibility of communication and the possibility of not being understood, the individual has already started on that long process of learning which makes it possible to talk of a "basic personality" common to members of a society. Within any social group or community patterns of child rearing usually vary very little. The sort of expectations and feelings set up by such patterns of rearing may be changed by later experience but, since it is usual for them to reflect a general pattern of living, they are more usually reinforced by later experiences. Since in general what comes early has a

[1] The term is borrowed from Kardiner, *The Individual and his Society*, Columbia University Press, New York (1939).

greater determining effect than what comes later, they have very considerable importance.

In general terms, for example, it is unusual for American and English children today to be carried around all the time (the odd child may be, but he is atypical); they are usually parked for large periods of the day in baby containers of one type or another; on the other hand, their freedom of movement is not usually grossly restricted though their vision may be. In some parts of the world, by contrast, children are automatically carried by an adult or an older child until they can at least sit up by themselves; in yet others they may be either swaddled or restricted in movement by being attached to a cradle board or some such other device. Again, feeding patterns vary enormously: some children are breastfed for three years, others for less than six months, some are given solid food from birth, others not till the second year or later. Some are fed when they cry, others left for very long periods between feedings. Some are toilet trained from birth, others not until they are four, or older. Some are bathed in hot water, some in cold, some in oil, and so on. The possibilities are very varied indeed, and all I can really do here is to point out the sort of differences and refer the reader elsewhere for details.[2]

There seem to be some absolute limits which control the range of possible variation and these are set by what the infant will survive in the way of handling. He is really remarkably accommodating, but he needs a certain amount of food, warmth, physical stimulation and affection to go on living; he may get the bare minimum of all of these, or he may get the near maximum. He may be taught deliberately quite a lot, or nothing at all. He may be regarded as extremely valuable, or as a nuisance. The child is born into a world which has an attitude towards him which is part of his earliest experience and so it is formative.

[2] Whiting, J. W. and Child, I. L., *Child Training and Personality*, Yale Univ. Press, New Haven (1953).

*Social learning in infancy*

Sooner or later in any culture, but usually very young, people begin in their turn to have expectations about the baby; there are things he "should" do and be. In most societies the elementary learning involved in being a member of the group is done before the age of five. Much of it is spontaneous learning involving little or no direct pressure to conform. But apart from this there is considerable learning by imitation and some which results from direct instigation. I shall leave a discussion of the more personal aspects of learning until Chapter IV, but want to consider here the range of social learning which is offered and demanded by any society. In our own society we expect children of five or six to show the rudiments of good manners; we expect them to say "hallo" and "goodbye", and "please" and "thank you", to shake hands, to endure being kissed by "aunty", to eat with implements; and those who do not accomplish this we think of as ill-mannered. This does not happen all at once, naturally; from the time a baby can sit up someone is usually urging it to wave bye-bye, or something like that. Now since children imitate easily and freely, much of this conventional social behaviour is learnt by imitation, but some of it is remorselessly ingrained by reiterated suggestion, coercion and bribery. But it would probably be learnt anyway if it was habitual and customary in adult behaviour—a lot of the rest comes under the heading of "making assurance doubly sure". Many social skills depend on the learning of speech, and again some of this speech is learnt not as meaning but as a social tool—a phrase or word which has a social function often at variance with its meaning, like the "How do you do?" which invites no reply; thus learning speech is a complex social skill as well as an intellectual one.

Children usually learn during these years the minimum standards of modesty demanded by society, and something of sex identification and sex rôle; societies vary very much in what sort of distinction they require between the sexes in behaviour and on the sort of behaviour comprehended under the notion of modesty—but no society appears to be lacking in either concept.

Since, during the same years, the child has to learn all sorts of physical and mental skills, one might think that it had enough to do, but the learning capacity at this time is apparently enormous. There is evidence that, in addition to learning the rudiments of conventional social behaviour, speech, locomotion, elimination control, self-feeding and so on, he also learns a great deal about what the world "ought to be", that is, the appropriate aesthetic tastes, the proper range of interests, what is edible or wearable, and about such everyday simple-minded things as washing up, dusting and looking at television. In other words, he learns in some global way the characteristics, standards and values of his social milieu.

## The formation of conscience

The only possible way in which one can account for the extent and range of such learning is through some process of unreflecting absorption, which is probably well called intro-jection by the psychoanalysts. This suggests a process of internalization of a model or models, so that the reference point for behaviour becomes internal rather than external. The child behaves, not as others demand, but as he comes to feel he demands or must. The most important aspect of this process is that which involves the development of a conscience, or super-ego, or what have you, whereby transgression of a code of behaviour produces guilt rather than fear of retribution. In normal people in any society such a process occurs—that it is a crude, non-rational process is easily seen by talking to children about their ideas of "good" and "bad", or by talking to adults who have retained the same sort of infantile con-science. In everyone some part of this process remains as the unconscious element of the super-ego, a permanent guardian of the *mores* of society. Since the "model" for this inter-nalization is familial, or cultural, the actual content of the instruction will vary from one culture to another, although there are undoubtedly elements so common as to be nearly certainly universal. This inner guide to behaviour makes social living possible; if there are no policemen inside, then you need more policemen than people to keep society going. But it is a crude process and often caricatures the built-in model, phantasy and distortion giving it a binding quality which the external law never has. The very primitive guilt involved in this process gives rise to all sorts of magical and superstitious behaviour designed to placate or ward off the threat felt by the transgressor. In most societies, again, devices of this kind are conventionalized in one way or another, and the child learns these conventional guilt assuagers along with how to feel guilty. In the normal course of events experience and reason modify in later life this primitive given conscience which the child acquires in its early years, but the essential process itself occurs early.

Since taste changes, the child may alter what he prefers as he grows up—but before he starts school he has acquired really all the essentials of cultural membership. He has done this in an, as yet, elementary way; his grip on the social situation may be as tenuous as his emotional control, his speech and thinking limited, particularly in abstract concepts, his taste arbitrary and vacillating, his dependence still very great, but he has an idea of "ought" which spreads beyond conduct to things and events. He is coming to an age when he can do some of his thinking for himself, he can take independent action which is not unreflecting even if the reflection is not very effective. During the later years of childhood he practises and perfects these human skills, he embarks on formal learning, whether of an academic or practical kind; whether he learns to read or to hunt, to weave or solve equations, will depend on what offers.

## Social learning in childhood

Once these early years are past, the child is over both his most vulnerable years physically and psychologically and his period of most rapid and essential learning. He is too immature to cope with life on his own, but in some measure he is set into the mould of social membership. To say that experience cannot change a child and his way of life after this age is palpably ridiculous, but he is certainly past his most formative years; what he learns thereafter will be more chosen and less simply absorbed from his surroundings without reflection that it might be otherwise. He has been asking "why" for years, but for information, for attention, for social comfort, more than from an interest in the dynamics of things—clearly children differ in this respect; a highly intelligent three-year-old will have more intellectual curiosity than a dull six-year-old, but it is a question of rate rather than mode of development.

In societies which have very little to offer in the way of variety of experience and skill, the child may have completed most of his essential social learning by the time he is five or six. Where methods of agriculture are simple and household techniques primitive, young children are quite as capable as adults in carrying out essential tasks though they may lack their strength and endurance. Even in societies where the level of technical skill is low, attitudes towards children differ; in some they work, in many they act as baby-minders, in still others they are left to their own devices till adolescence. Almost every possible different attitude towards later childhood that one can think of is exemplified in some society, present or past. In this the human species differs markedly from most animal groups. In animals the pattern of social training differs little from one community to another; in people it differs so much as almost to defy classification.

But there is another aspect to social learning and this has to do with ritual, ceremony and cult. The amount of learning demanded of a child in this respect varies again very greatly. In some, such training begins in babyhood: among the Bali, for example, children are taught dance movements almost before they can walk. In many pre-literate societies children are taught tribal legends, genealogies, ritual songs and exact accounts of the correct method of carrying out rarely used skills, from early childhood. In many, such training is delayed till adolescence, at which time elaborate puberty ceremonials and initiation rites are accompanied by periods devoted to the learning of essential tribal law, legends and ceremonial. In still others, like our own, there is no special time for such training, and ritual becomes the specialized province of the few; ceremonies are mostly confined to the religious ones concerned with birth, marriage and death, and other learning of custom is casual, or confined to formal education which differs greatly from place to place and class to class.

## Society as the framework for life

Whether such training is calculated and exact, or largely haphazard, in some way or another the society within which a person grows up provides him with a framework for living, an interpretation of life, a set of laws and values which both tell him the appropriate thing to do in a wide variety of circumstances and the things which he may not do without peril, social, physical or religious. In addition, in almost all societies he is given an opportunity to learn a number of specialized skills—in advanced societies there may be a wide choice of these, in smaller and more primitive communities he may learn them all. But whether he learns to hunt caribou or play the clarinet, to cure skins or make pottery, a store of knowledge and skill is passed on from one generation to the next which enables the gifted members of a society to add something in each generation. When a society is widely literate this opportunity is immensely expanded, since the individual can call on a vast store of knowledge rather than rely on the amount he can commit to memory.

In any society skills may be lost from one generation to another rather than gained; in times of war, famine, invasion, such loss of skill is typical, but humanity being what it is something is usually salvaged from the wreck in the form of artifacts, or written records, which allow for the re-establishment of such skills if they are interesting or useful. Such records of past achievement may be lost or neglected for long periods, but they accumulate just the same, and they form the cultural inheritance of the world. How much any individual member of the human race receives of that cultural inheritance depends on accidents of birth, education and intelligence, but no one grows to maturity in society without falling heir to some portion of it.

The earliest years of life are those in which the child absorbs the fundamentals of his culture, its language, emotional dispositions, and something of its outlook through the medium of his immediate family, and learning is inescapable, unreflective and to some extent irreversible. In later childhood comes a period of broadening horizons, in which the child, freed from something of his early dependence, is increasingly interested in the world around him; this is a period in which formal learning becomes possible. He learns during these years much of what the society offers in the way of practical and social skills; in such learning, direct understanding, voluntary effort and some degree of genuine choice are involved. Though still limited in great part by what is available, the child begins to exercise some degree of independent judgement and selection among the possibilities to hand. When adolescence is reached, the last period of learning is entered upon, and typically the child becomes capable of a much greater degree of intellectual independence; since abstract ideas come to interest him in their own right, he may come to question the values and outlook, even the *mores*, of his society.

The capacity for reflective thought is developed, even if it is never called into play. The adolescent enters a phase in which he acts upon his society and is less completely acted upon by it. Whether he adds anything, or merely reflects what he has been brought up to be, will depend on many other things but in some measure upon himself. Once the person is adult his period of social and cultural learning is virtually over. What he learns from this point on, or whether he learns at all, will depend on the sort of person he is rather than his stage of development. When a culture is forced to change rapidly, either because of social or technological change within it, or pressure from without, the older the person is the less easy it will be for him to adapt to such change. He carries within him a completed conception of the world around him as it ought to be, and if it differs too much from this he may acquire a veneer of the new way of life, or acquiesce in it, but he will seldom feel truly a part of it—which is one of the reasons why the old "never know what the world is coming to". This setting of the culture within the individual preserves the way of life within the culture, gives it its stability and durability—what effect this has on the society will depend upon circumstances, but the idea that one must "catch people young" if one wants materially to alter their outlook on life is a truism.

## WHAT THE CULTURE DEMANDS

### Society as a mode of life

A culture gives the person the mode of expressing his humanity—it is the mould which determines in a large measure what he thinks and feels, what he likes and dislikes, what he may do, what he wants to do, what he is able to do. To say that society makes us what we are is not to deny our ability to be ourselves, but to emphasize that we can only operate in, and through, society if we are to be people at all. To claim independence of society is fair enough provided that we remember that we do so in language and in reference to a particular way of life or set of possibilities. This is not to say that we cannot reject or withdraw our support from particular aspects of society, but that we usually do so selectively or, alternatively, we abandon our own society in order to join another community. In a very minor way, for example, we may revolt against the habit of eating boiled cabbage, and decide that we will eat it no more; we may try to stop others eating it without placing the same embargo on potatoes. Or we may decide to go

and live in a part of the world where boiled cabbage is unknown and hence cease to eat it because we now live in a
society where mangoes are common rather than cabbage. But
each of these possibilities occurs within a social context, has a
social significance even though these are widely different in
range and extent. We live within a social context, and we carry
it with us even when no one is around; we achieve our measure
of independence within society in the widest sense, even when
we stray beyond its acknowledged bounds in either space or
conduct.

What we need to make clear here is a distinction between a
*modus operandi* and an action, between technique and execu-
tion. To say that no one can write a poem without words,
images, ideas and some sense of rhythm is a very far call from
saying any individual poem is not original, good, inspiring or
the reverse. The copyist, the plagiarist, the writer of pot-
boilers, merely make use of what is around—so does the
creative artist, but the difference is one we can all recognize.
To be effective most forms of creative original work must
achieve a measure of communication, or they lack social relevance and personal significance. The audience may be small,
but it must exist at least hypothetically. It is easier to see this
principle in the creative arts but it applies in many areas of
life. The reference points for many of our activities are social,
the techniques we employ are learned in society, but this does
not necessarily stamp them with the hallmark of social conformity. Again, originality is easier to see in the startlingly
novel than in the everyday actions of those about us, but
actually nearly everything we do and say has elements of both
repetition and originality.

### The problem of originality

The thing that usually seems more obvious is that much
originality is unimportant because the main course of the
action, or statement, is expected or conventional. We probably
never get on a bus in quite the same way as the time before,

but we do so near enough to excite no comment; there is a range within which we perform that we could call the limits of expected variation. The same is true with conversations which often serve ends other than direct communication from mind to mind. But when we have a mindless conversation it must be conducted within limits; it must be variable, approximately meaningful and not obviously mechanical; this might seem a considerable demand, but one most people can easily meet while thinking of something different, or of nothing at all. The listener is equally "mindless" unless a discordant note creeps in. This one might call the vigilance aspect of the situation, and in it we include the apprehension of omissions as well as the inclusion of expected content. What we usually mean by original is something outside this expected range of variation, something which focuses our attention whether in approbation, disgust, distress or merely surprise. Unless we understand this it is very difficult to account for the variety in sameness which makes up much of our lives.

It can be shown that for most people absolute repetition of movements, speech and so on is distressing to all but the very dim, but then people's capacity to tolerate the really novel is also limited. Much of the popular art illustrates this principle very well[3] and it accounts much better for normal human behaviour than an idea of habit as a rigid pattern of action. The conformity which society is often said to demand of the individual takes much more the form that he is not expected to act, think, or feel, outside a prescribed range of variation, than that he is expected to do any very specific set of things; though this latter element is easier to tabulate and describe than the more elastic but just as binding limits set by the expectancies of his friends and neighbours. If your female child becomes a secretary you do not in our society have to "explain" it to the neighbours, but if she becomes a member of a harem, or a boxing champion, it will raise eyebrows here and there.

[3] Harding, D. W., "The Social Background of Taste in Music", *The Musical Times* (1938), Nos. 1143 and 1144.

## The demand for the expected

That which can be neither understood, expected, nor explained tends to be seen as lacking in social relevance, perhaps as mad, funny, wicked, but definitely unacceptable; though the inexplicable, too, can with time come within the range of the expected, so that the person is expected to be unexpected, nonconformist, unconventional or whatever it is. The power of these social forces and social weapons should not be underestimated; they, more than obvious external demands, constitute the pressure to conformity within society. They allow the individual a measure of liberty and a measure of security. Complex as such systems are, they depend so much on early learning and habit that they demand little conscious reflection, little effort, except in unusual circumstances. They are also an easy route to much mental indolence, hypocrisy and timeserving because they save so much trouble and are so genuinely useful. The enormous complexity of this system of responses defies complete analysis, but the principles appear to hold whenever a particular aspect is selected for study. Among common examples of things included in the expectancy systems are habits of speech, table manners, fashions in clothes and popular songs; although most of these are almost peripheral elements compared with the flow of speech and action that surrounds us, they are good microcosms in which to observe the wider principle.

In the ordinary course of events people have detailed expectations about people they know well, and are correspondingly indignant if they act "out of character". People have expectancies for classes of people, with some of which they may identify themselves, but also about others they feel to be different. Such expectancies may take on a very formal character and are then usually described as stereotypes.[4] When experience fails to correspond with expectation, the stereotype

[4] Gordon, R., "Some factors that favour the formation of stereotyped images", *Brit. J. Psychol.* (1949), **39**, 156–77.

often wins out, the actual experience being dismissed as exceptional. Stereotypes may be associated with a high degree of negative feeling which we describe as prejudice (although the word can equally be used of positive feeling, the overtone seems to be changing in the negative direction). These prejudiced expectancies may be rigid but are seldom detailed in the way that those about our friends are. The larger and more remote the unit we deal with the less detailed the expectations on the whole. The most remote and vague are about classes or groups of people of whom you "don't know what to expect", except perhaps that they are likely to be different.

## The authoritarian character

Critical social attitudes thus conform to certain general laws which override the specific material dealt with; but within the broad framework thus provided we have to note differences between both individuals and societies. Individuals differ considerably in the extent to which they are bound by their expectancies, by the degree of narrowness and rigidity which these exhibit on the one hand, and by the number and range of them on the other. Those in whom stereotyping is common, flexibility of outlook small, have been in an extensive and careful study[5] called authoritarian characters and contrasted with a more flexible democratic type. In considering the general conclusions that prejudice, racial, religious and social, is characteristic of the authoritarian character, we have to recognize the possibility of a degree of prejudice among psychologists as a group against people of this type. They may be the prototype of the wicked, but the tenor of these commentators is not without overtones of the "I can tolerate anything but intolerance" attitude, itself prone to irrationality. In some of these studies there has been a quite insufficient attempt to distinguish the characteristic mode of thought from its content and a certain blurring of judgement. With all that there is

[5] Adorno, T. N. and others, *The Authoritarian Personality*, Harper, New York (1950).

enough evidence to warrant the distinction, and to show that the authoritarian attitude is much more characteristic of some subgroups in society than of others.[6] In such groups, it would appear, attitudes are fostered which allow only narrow limits to expectancy systems for compatible people, and view those outside this immediate group in largely unfavourable terms, the whole picture being one of arbitrary classification of people and a general harshness towards non-conformity.

## Difference and change

But to pick up the other thread, the number and range of expectancy systems vary as well as their type. Where education and experience are limited and society is very uniform, the range of expectancies may be small, except for recognized sub-grouping (say by age, wealth, occupation, family) within the community, and vague "other" attitudes. On the other hand, sophisticated people in a complex society may have an enormous range of both classifications and expectancies. This range is cut across by the authoritarian attitude: it is possible to be prejudiced in a very complex and extensive way, or equally to be tolerant in the same terms. What education and experience can do is to widen the range of situations, and people, with which a person is able to cope easily and effectively, to enable him to find which of his general expectancies are valid in most situations and which particular, which limited experience will prevent him from knowing. A knowledge that other people's attitudes differ widely from one's own may seem self-evident, but the form of these differences is not always predictable, and in the social sciences some notable examples of errors of this kind serve as warnings of the perils of assuming too much.[7]

[6] It should be borne in mind that most of these studies are carried out in America, and only limited repetitions elsewhere; the studies are hence culture-tied and might need reformulation for cross-cultural use.

[7] A classical and probably apocryphal example is usually quoted in illustration of this point. Someone attempting to test the intelligence of children in a North American tribe found that they were apparently

Changes in "the acceptable" come about in two ways, most often by a slight stretching of the limits of the distribution, adding to the range of the possible, or expected, bit by bit, or by the gradual eroding of expectations; such changes we hardly notice until we look back and find the old range queer, dated, or outmoded. And the other more unusual way is through major upheaval, a process usually bitterly resisted by those who accept the slower process without noticing it much. Any radical challenge to the accepted conventions meets an equally radical resistance both in the individual and in society. But there is a graduated system of expectancies which means that the context in which a novel idea occurs will determine whether it is seen as a challenge towards change, an enlightenment, interesting or irrelevant. This means that the whole thing is even more complicated, since the systems of expectancy are themselves dynamic and expanding and at the same time conservative and change-resisting. Analysing the pattern of this aspect of any social group is a first requirement for those hoping to carry out successful propaganda campaigns, or programmes of indoctrination, or even advertising, since these are successful in so far as they can add something to the expectancy gestalt. ("People at the top not only have all the characteristics you would expect, but they also carry brief cases made by X" will work as advertising, but "people at the top always carry sub-machine guns by Y" will not work, because it is too far from the rest of the expectancy pattern.) In the ordinary course of events successful propaganda should extend rather than affront, or, if a challenge is included, it should be of the shock-followed-by-reassurance type, but the very sophistication of this latter technique makes it suitable only for an equally sophisticated audience.

---

unable to solve the simplest problem; this puzzled him considerably, until he found out that they had been brought up to consider it very rude to know the answers to questions which adults did not—they found him remarkably ill-informed!

## The demand for conformity

Just as individuals differ and social subgroups differ so do cultures, some having much greater emphasis on conformity than others, some allowing a much wider range of experience than others. There are cultures in which a degree of homogeneity may be virtually imposed by the physical circumstances of living, but even here some offer a wider range of possible rôles than others. No society is so homogeneous that everyone is expected to be the same as everyone else, but the possible distinctions may be many or few, clearly or loosely defined. Proliferation of rôle and opportunities to differ are nearly always the mark of a technologically advanced society whose numbers are large and in which a degree of mobility is possible. It has been argued that non-conformity is a political and economic luxury, but it depends entirely on what you mean by this whether it is true. The pressure to conformity can be quite as great in a modern suburb as in a simple fishing community—it may even be greater[8] because it can be more efficient. It is certainly more likely to be felt as pressure when other possibilities are perceived.

But it is a mistake to see all the pressures to conformity as coming from without—many come from within; "keeping up with the Joneses" is a well known social habit, the horror of being found in a bathing suit at a dinner party in town perceptible to most. Reisman has postulated that cultures differ in this respect also.[9] He suggests people may be either inner-directed, outer-directed or other-directed, relying for their directions for behaviour on internalized standards, tradition or other people respectively. He suggests that the American pattern of life is "other directed", European patterns variously inner or outer directed. Although he undoubtedly exaggerated in order to make the impact of his theory clearer, there is

[8] Whyte, W., *The Organization Man*, Simon & Schuster, New York (1956).

[9] Riesman, D., *The Lonely Crowd*, Yale Univ. Press, New Haven (1953).

obviously considerable difference between societies and periods of history in the extent to which people draw their guides to proper behaviour from each of these three sources. In a stable society under no particular external threat, tradition may govern most aspects of life; in an immigrant society, such as the U.S.A. once had, it would be minimally useful; a missionizing or colonizing society on the other hand would put inner-directed people at a premium. It may well be that in all societies types are mixed, but the best adapted are prominent, successful and seen as the model for the society in the eyes of the others.

## Cultural relativism

All of this has to do with what might be called the overall mechanisms for creating and maintaining social attitudes and habits within a social group. But we must go a little further and examine something of the content of the ideas, values, expectations and actions which are the life within these rather theoretical bones. What are people's expectations, what are the attitudes or values they hold rigidly and what is it they feel to be proper or improper in human behaviour? It was fashionable in the earlier part of this century to suggest that the possibilities here were indefinite, that what was good or bad, proper or improper, was particular to a society, that in so far as the individual conformed to the norm for that society he was ethically adequate.

Social relativism influenced many psychologists, among them rather notably Piaget;[10] Ruth Benedict in *Patterns of Culture*[11] drew the same sort of conclusion from anthropological rather than sociological data. Eric Fromm has elaborated the psychological arguments for such a viewpoint[12] in his discussion of the moral growth of the individual and

[10] Piaget, J., *The Moral Judgement of the Child*, Trench & Trubner, London (1932).

[11] Benedict, R., *Patterns of Culture*, Routledge, London (1935).

[12] Fromm, E., *Man for Himself*, Routledge & Kegan Paul, London (1950).

society. Roughly described as cultural relativism, this point of view contrasts both with a traditional view that absolute values can be found in any dimension, to which peoples and individuals do or do not approximate, and the progressive or evolutionist view that the whole of human culture is proceeding towards some as yet unrealized set of values, but what hinders progress is bad, and what forwards it is good. It is important to realize that any real degree of detachment is rare in this field— the majority of writers have had social, political or philosophical axes to grind and are well aware of this.

Probably one of the most objective and well argued discussions of this field is that given by Harding[13] who concludes that, while the area of cultural relativism is great, there are some ways of life and values which are better than others in that they are recognizably better to live in, more congruent with man's nature, more fitted to his needs. To adopt such a view it is necessary to take some criterion such as happiness, stick one's neck out, and say that this is the appropriate yardstick and other people can take it or leave it. It is something one can argue for but hardly prove in any strong sense. If one does take such a measure, then it follows that a sick society is one in which most people are miserable, and a healthy society one in which most people are fairly happy. Both common observation and the literature of social anthropology and psychology make it clear that some people are quite clearly happier than others, and certain conditions of life are more conducive to this state than others. To conclude that there are limits to the "arc of human potentiality" (to use Ruth Benedict's phrase) seems logical; or at least to conclude that some portions of that "arc" are more fitting than others to the nature of man.

### Universal human values

This is one aspect of the problem; there is another: in spite of the very great diversity of customs, *mores* and laws which

[13] Harding, D. W., *Social Psychology and Individual Values*, Hutchinson, London (1953).

human societies exhibit, there is some evidence of convergence in ideas about what is good[14] and bad in the way of action, certain universals of a very broad kind which are essential to the maintenance of a community. Two outstanding examples of undesirable actions are murder and incest. Societies differ greatly in how to define either category of behaviour, but they recognize some form of them. Murder may be defined very broadly as the taking of any human life, or, much more narrowly, as the taking of particular lives outside recognized limits, for example in some communities ritual "murder" may be proper, while other kinds are taboo. In a great many societies the killing of enemy prisoners is not regarded as murder, in yet others it is customary to kill the weak, deformed or mentally deficient. In the majority of societies, but not all, killing in war or in self defence is not seen as murder; but the differences arise in what might be called exempt categories rather than in the basic notion. Societies again differ very greatly in the sanctions they impose on a murderer: in some they merely watch him and stop him doing it again if they can; in others they require a murderer (if male) to marry his victim's wife; in yet others they kill the murderer (this does not count as murder), and so on.

Incest taboos are likewise various. They nearly always involve the prohibition of marriage between closely related people, but there the similarity ends. In the majority of societies sexual relations between parents and offspring are regarded as incestuous, but even this is not universal. In some societies you must marry your cousins, in others you must not. In some you may marry your father's cousin but not your mother's—the complications are endless, but the general drift is to prevent marriage among those closely related by blood. Transgression

[14] Perhaps the most interesting of all is that people can make sense of "good" as an idea in all languages; what they mean by it may differ but a "better idea of good" seems possible to most people; thus the scale on which the value is judged is to some extent independent of its current contents.

of incest rules may be controlled by various social punishments, but is commonly seen as offending against supernatural agencies and associated with guilt, as well as offending the self image and so associated with shame. The Oedipus myth sums up in one neat story the general theme of most murder and incest taboos.

Attitudes towards property are more variable but some notion of mine and thine seems widespread, although what is so defined may vary from personal ornaments to copyright or include both. Wide differences are observed in the extent to which property is held in common by the group, or the family, or particularly by the individual or by no one.[15] The modes by which property is inherited are so many and so complicated that, beyond saying that property is usually disposed of by some system acknowledged within a particular society, little generalization is possible. Any society which is interested in personal property usually has a clear code covering its disposal on the death of the owner; in some simple societies this may involve its burial with the remains of its owner, but usually it is more involved than this.

On the other hand, what is regarded as theft in some societies is regarded as clever in others, and nearly every group recognizes things which it feels it is "right" to take, whether this is land in a colonizing nation, weapons, women and goods in warring nations, or other ill-gotten gains in more organized societies. Differences in codes on what constitutes theft are extremely subtle and very difficult to understand in societies other than one's own because they seldom have an extrinsic logic, but that is another story altogether.

About areas of agreement it is difficult to be so specific; things like loyalty and treachery, sacrilege and reverence are widely understood but differ greatly in action and meaning from place to place. Other things still are quite clearly culture-

---

[15] The "by no one" idea is positive because it implies that no one can lay claim to its exclusive use—colonizing nations find this concept quite meaningless if their usual behaviour is anything to go by.

tied—it is proper to boast in one society and taboo in another, in some places kindness is a good thing, in others it is equated with feebleness and failure. The only thing one can safely say is that nearly all the virtues and vices are observable in every human community only sometimes they shift categories in a rather startling way.

The individual in society, then, is subject to what might be called the pressures of expectation and the objective rules of life in that society. He in his turn exerts the same sort of influence on the other members. But since within any society he may by accident of birth or upbringing have very different rights, privileges and duties, he will be subject to particular as well as general demands. The over-riding demand of any social group is towards moderated conformity—without this the group would simply fragment. But as an important part of this social demand system there is a continuous process whereby new situations are evaluated and judged by a dialogue which strives towards a consensus of opinion about what is the correct way of coping, the right way to behave, the proper way to act and so forth. Even the most tyrannical dictator cannot act too far away from what people will assent to, otherwise he stops being a dictator and probably becomes a corpse. Societies are not static receptacles of ideas and actions, but dynamic units within which people constantly strive to maintain particular sets of values and ways of behaving through a process which involves more than the nominal assent of particular individuals. Some individuals may be negligible in this process but, whatever the political organization, no substantial dissenting body is in the long run totally without influence.

# PART II

# MAN AS AN INDIVIDUAL

# CHAPTER III

# THE BASIS OF
# INDIVIDUALITY

## PSYCHO-GENETICS

### Genetic identity

No two people are precisely the same. Most of us differ in heredity from one another in some degree with the rare exception of identical twins. Still more does our experience differ; even twins who are reared together[1] cannot be picked up at the same time by the same person with the same hand. The importance of our uniqueness is debatable, but it certainly appears to each of us to be a matter of considerable personal significance.

Just how much we differ from one another is much harder to say; it is harder still to be sure how much of the differences we see are genetic in origin. As we observe the differences in people around us they have their origin in both genetic and constitutional[2] factors and in the influences of the physical and cultural

[1] The reason that psychologists so often seem obsessively bent on the pursuit of identical twins "reared together" or "reared apart" is the unique opportunity they provide for the study of heredity.

[2] Constitutional characteristics which are not heritable are usually defects of some kind which arise as a result of some interference with the growth processes before birth, or from damage during or soon after birth. "Thalidomide babies" suffer irreversible constitutional damage which is not heritable. Similarly, children with congenital syphilis suffer damage which is contracted by infection from the mother but is not

environment in which the individual has grown to maturity. The various factors at work may cancel one another out or act cumulatively to increase the differences attributable to any one of them. One thing is certain, the extent of such observable differences is very variable. In small isolated populations sharing a common culture and a common language superficial differences may be very small though they are never absent; in such cases the gene pool[3] is likely to be rather limited, as well as the opportunities for varied experience; both factors together make for comparative homogeneity. By contrast, in a technologically advanced culture which allows, indeed demands, diversity of experience and in which there are wider possibilities of intermarriage and so a less limited gene pool, the differences may be seen to be very great.

What can we say of the heritable aspects of such differences as are observed? Most of our knowledge of genetics is derived from the study of physical characteristics in animals and men. Clear differences in hair type, hair and eye colour, and blood groups we are familiar with, but these concern us less here than such questions as whether temperamental and personality characteristics are heritable, together with intelligence and other special abilities and aptitudes and, finally, that vexed problem of the inheritance of acquired characteristics.

## The mechanism of differential inheritance

This is not the place to write at length about the theory of genetics; all I can do is to ask the reader to bear in mind that

---

itself inherited. Where such damage occurs in early critical stages of growth it is usually irreversible in the individual, but properly speaking the defect is acquired and not inherited.

[3] The "gene pool" is a way of describing the number of variant genes available in the breeding population; thus if there are theoretically, say, ten possible colours of hair, and in any population only one or two of these are actually present, none of the others can in the normal course of events occur, and we say that the gene pool is more limited than if all ten possibilities occurred in that population.

such theory is complex and liable to revision.[4] A few things, though, must be made clear: the first is that there is every evidence that the mechanism of inheritance is basically the same for all species; details differ, but the broad outline is general, therefore cross-species generalization is less dangerous in this field than in almost any other. The second important point is that between genotype (the actual genetic constitution) and phenotype (the manifest characteristics) many factors and situations intervene in any animal which takes a long time to reach maturity. Height is in general genetically determined, but malnutrition and illness may result in a failure of the organism to reach its full height. That is to say that once again we have to do with a very complex series of interactions; there seems to be a general limiting condition set by heredity, but the determination is not absolute. Granted identical rearing conditions of a minimally favourable kind, individual differences due to heredity will be seen most clearly, but differences in genotype (or genetic constitution) can be effectively masked in the adult organism in a number of ways.

The last point is that many genetically determined differences are of an all-or-none type, that is, if you have black hair it does not suddenly go blond (or not without aid), although it may well, and indeed probably will, go grey. Such characteristics are frequently used as illustrations of the mendelian principles of genetics and follow these fairly well on the whole. But other genetically controlled characteristics exhibit what is known as continuous variation—something you have more or less of but everyone has in some degree (for example, height again). Such continuously variable characteristics often have a "normal" distribution, that is, one in which the majority of people are close to the average for a population with fewer and fewer individuals showing the more extreme ranges of the characteristic.

[4] The latest important advance has been through an understanding of the way in which DNA codes genetic information or instructions; a good readable account of this can be found in *The Scientific American* (1962), Vol. 206, No. 1, page 20, in an article entitled "The Fine Structure of the Gene" by Benzer, S.

Such continuous variation can come about in several ways: it can be because a large number of genes[5] combine to produce the effect (for example, piebalding in mice), or because some genes exert a modifying influence on others when both are present, or because the observed effect is so distant from the determining one that the two or more distinct genotypes become obscured by the effort of other intervening influences.[6] There remains the possibility that there are no genetic determinants in such variation; they arise in a genetically identical population as a result of varied experience. It is virtually impossible to decide which of these conditions in fact prevails without experiment, and since genetic experiments with people are impractical or impossible[7] we have to proceed with great caution and largely by inference and analogy when postulating the genetic determinants of human variation.

## Mental inheritance

In psychogenetics[8] we have to deal largely with traits which exhibit continuous variation and appear, at least with the measuring devices we use, to be normally distributed. The whole topic is surrounded by controversy, there being little agreement even on so basic an issue as whether there is any proper sense in which we may talk of psycho-genetics at all.

[5] This assumes that the "gene" is the basic genetic unit, an assumption which is reasonable as a working hypothesis.

[6] A good example of this is given by Penrose in his discussion of the relation between phenylketonuria and intelligence in "Measurement of pleiotropic effects in phenylketonuria", *Ann. Eugen. London* (1951), **16**, 134–41.

[7] They have a very long life span which makes it difficult to study enough generations and even more it is usually impossible to control their mating patterns (for ethical, political and purely practical reasons), so that you have to wait upon the "chance" occurrence of the genetic combinations that you wish to study.

[8] A word coined to describe that area of genetics which has to do with the inheritance of psychological rather than physical attributes; some authors prefer "behaviour genetics" but on the whole I think this last term may suggest a rather restricted field of inquiry and prefer what I consider to be the broader term.

On the one hand we have a school of thought deriving from Watson's[9] extreme statement and continuing through other behaviourists to a modern exponent in Skinner, which argues that there is no such thing as mental inheritance, that all differences in temperament and ability result from experience. They have argued that we may inherit differences in anatomical structure and sensory sensitivity, but that is the absolute limit. A good deal of the ground for such a position is cut from under their feet by evidence gathered from the study of animals, but that does not seem to worry them much. At the other extreme there are people who go so far as to suggest that not only the broad lines of temperament, ability and mental illness are heritable, but even criminal tendencies. This position is seldom taken today in so extreme a form among reputable psychologists, first because the evidence for it is poor and secondly because its social and political implications are alarming, but people still argue that body type, and with it predictable associated patterns of behaviour, is inherited, or that neurotic conditions are inherited. In general we can say that this is a subject which seems to call forth rather extreme statements and which requires careful and critical thinking, and perhaps a great deal more evidence than we have at present, if we are to avoid brash partisan polemics which owe more to emotional conviction than to scientific accuracy.

## HERITABLE DIFFERENCES IN KIND

### Mental abnormalities

It is useful to make a distinction between those characteristics which can be called discrete, that is, which appear to be different in kind, and those which are continuously distributed, that is, different in degree; and nearly all of these discrete characteristics are abnormalities of one kind or another. So far as psychological characteristics are concerned there are remarkably few examples of the all-or-none (differences in kind)

[9] Watson, J. B., *op. cit.*

type of genetic distinctions; among those that we know the majority are cases in which the psychological condition is secondary to a much more distinct metabolic or neurological peculiarity. Certain rare forms of mental deficiency can be shown to be inherited, though not in the simple sense that defective parents produce defective offspring.[10] Probably the best documented example of a disease process of this kind is Huntingdon's Chorea, which has a known genetic background, but is itself a very rare condition. The only other important case of what appears to be an all-or-none characteristic which may have a genetic background is provided by certain types of severe mental illness. Although it is arguable that psychotic[11] illness is a matter of degree, it is much less obviously true than the idea that we are all more or less neurotic. There appears to be at any rate a good case for saying that the presence or absence of psychosis constitutes a difference in kind psychologically.

There is evidence that schizophrenia[12] and possibly some of the depressive illnesses (conditions which are more or less verifiably present or absent), are heritable.[13] But the heritability appears to take the form of an unusual predisposition to those

[10] The genetic mechanism in such conditions nearly always seems to be a pair of recessive genes. When both parents carry the recessive, although neither will show it, some 25 per cent of their children will show the defect. In nearly all cases these children will be sterile or never reach puberty. The probability can be altered by other factors which may give a higher rate of incidence; further, such a figure as 25 per cent. represents an average probability (in a population with the relevant characteristics), in some families none of the children will be affected, in others all. The human family is too small for an expected ratio to work out exactly.

[11] Psychosis: Mental illness severe enough to prevent the patient from living a normal life; he may be a danger to himself and others in the acute stages of such illness. Roughly, conditions that in popular speech are known as "insanity".

[12] Schizophrenia: An illness characterized by loss of contact with reality and hallucinations; commonly occurring in late adolescence or early adulthood.

[13] Kallman, F. J., *Heredity in Health and Mental Disorder*, Norton, New York (1953), gives a good account of the available evidence.

illnesses rather than an inevitable outcome, as is the case with Huntingdon's Chorea. We need to exercise here rather more than usual caution, because the argument tends to become obscured by the amount of emotion such matters evoke. The situation is complicated by the fact that schizophrenic parents are less likely than persons without that illness to be able to provide adequate psychological care for their children, and the absence of such care does in itself seem to be a causative factor in the illness. But the evidence for a hereditary predisposition to such illness seems nevertheless convincing. It seems worthwhile to say, in passing, that the more we come to understand the precise course of the disease process the better we shall be able to provide for prevention and cure of the disease.

## Sex-linked differences

In all human communities there are the basic biological and psychological differences imposed by sexual distinction. This distinction is one of kind, genetically controlled through a known mechanism; it can be asked whether this basic genetic difference has ramifications in psychology as well as biology. There are two ways in which psychological traits may be associated with sexual differential. Such characteristics might arise more or less directly from the primary sex difference, that is, be part of the total pattern, or they might be genetically distinct from these but sex-linked. The first possibility is given some support by studies with animals which suggest that the behavioural patterns appropriate to both sexes are latent in both, but differences in hormone production determine which are manifest.[14] This does not rule out the second possibility, or indeed the third, that no such psychological implications are involved in sexual distinction.

In the human race, as opposed to some other species, but in common with the higher apes, sexual differentiation is not physically marked beyond the major sex organs and some rela-

[14] Beach, F. A., *Hormones and Behaviour*, Hoeber, London (1948).

tively minor secondary sex characteristics. This may seem trite, but in insects in particular the structural differences between males and females may be very great in terms both of size, shape, colouring and so on. In many species of birds the colouring of the males and females is sufficiently distinct to appear more striking at first view than many inter-specific differences. In mammals such sharp distinctions in physique are less common—though certain striking secondary sex characteristics in the way of tusks, antlers and so on are observed—many of these being subject to seasonal variation which is associated with seasonal variation in sexual activity.

In man there are a number of sex-linked phenomena which are sometimes associated with sexual differentiation. We are more familiar with those which might be described as physical handicaps than with examples which have a happier connotation. Haemophilia is a good example of such a sex-linked characteristic; it commonly occurs in the male though passed on by a female in whom it is not apparent. The most common form of colour blindness is sex-linked in the same way—it affects something like one male in twelve but only one female in 200—although again commonly passed on by the female. Baldness in the male is another sad example. So far as more precisely psychological characteristics are concerned, it is held by many authorities that both genius and mental defect are more common in the male than the female, but the evidence is controversial and the dispute bitter as to whether this is really true or, if thought true, attributable to cultural influences rather than constitutional factors.

More direct consequences of the sexual distinction, such as are to be seen for example in the extensive work done on the heritability of aggression in rats and mice, have to some extent been neglected. Nearly all the experimental animals in such studies are males, because it has been found that male rats and mice are more readily stirred to unprovoked violence towards one another than females of the same species. In other words, this latter difference has apparently been too obvious to be worth more than passing attention. Yet even among rodents further exploration of this male-female difference can give rise to a good deal of interesting material. The difference seems to be not so much one of absolute pugnacity (if there is such a thing), but rather what sort of situation will make them fight. This means that a relatively simple explanation of the difference based on the difference in hormone output is not quite sufficient.

We are concerned here with a complex pattern involving not only type of stimulus and the threshold at which stimuli become effective, but also the general patterning of the animal's behaviour in terms of its needs, purposes and goals. So far as I know, no one has fully explored the neurological and endocrine background of such differences, partly because the differences themselves have been so sketchily studied; but there is, as has already been suggested, a considerable body of evidence that patterns of sexual behaviour appropriate to the male and female are latent in both sexes and the endocrine balance determines which are manifest. Outside this specifically sexual area differences between the sexes in behavioural dispositions have not been fully explored even in animals.

In man the picture is infinitely more complex since the demands and pressures of culture seem to be so important in establishing appropriate patterns of behaviour for the sexes. Some cultural anthropologists[15] have gone so far as to suggest that there are no inherent differences in temperament or ability between the male and female, all those one witnesses being a product of cultural pressures. But such a view seems to be only partly supported by the evidence offered; it contains both contradictions and anomalies, and allows nothing at all for possible genetic peculiarities in some of the populations studied. We are left then with a certain body of evidence from animal studies that males and females differ in temperament as well as sexual characteristics and so a strong probability exists that

[15] E.g. Mead, M., *Male and Female*, Gollancz, London (1949).

this may also be to some extent true of people—but rather incomplete evidence at this level. In view of the very long time which it takes people to mature, cultural pressures could offset relatively weak genetic predispositions, so that even the absence of observable, or measurable, differences cannot be taken as conclusive evidence either way.

In addition, the immediate physical characteristics of the sexes may confront them with experiences which lead almost inevitably to psychological differences without the latter being necessarily inherent. The greater physical strength of men may enable them to solve problems in a way that women could not; equally, the greater longevity and resistance to disease in women compared with men may confront them with a different life situation and hence a different response, leaving aside the more dramatic differences imposed by child bearing. These are relatively simple examples, but serve to illustrate the difficulty of analysing the factors involved in any observable difference of a psychological kind.

## HERITABLE DIFFERENCES IN DEGREE

### The inheritance of intelligence

Whatever their precise genetic origin, we are more commonly confronted in fact with differences in degree when we study the heritability of some psychological or behavioural trait. Occasionally one may suspect that apparently continuous gradation is an artifact and that the methods of measurement used are not the best imaginable ones, but we must look at the evidence in the form in which we find it even if we have such reservations. The nature of the problem can be best understood through a rather brief look at the evidence concerning intelligence. The amount of time and energy which has been devoted to a consideration of the differential inheritance of intelligence is considerable and the literature vast. Such investigations have been carried out in an atmosphere of great heat; the political and social implications have ensured that, and it is not surprising that the controversies have been perhaps more remarkable for their emotionality than their clarity. It sometimes seems that everything that can be argued here has been argued, and further evidence using the same methods will get us very little further.

When all the dust has settled it appears that (leaving aside gross mental deficiency[16]) heredity plays a fair part in determining differences in measurable intelligence. But before accepting any of the apparently precise figures which have been offered for the proportions attributed to heredity and environment it is well to stand back from the problem. "Intelligence" is measured in such studies with tests which have only reasonably good reliability[17]; in hard fact such measures, while good, are also rough. They will effectively divide a population into about five major groups, small differences cannot be regarded as important with any real justification. Further, they are culture tied, which means that, given that a population has the same sort of education and experience, differences require explanation in terms of heredity; but without that common experience the differences are virtually impossible to interpret. A good account of the evidence on this point is given in most elementary textbooks in psychology, and it leads us, on the whole, to a conclusion that considerable differences in intelligence can be attributed to heredity, but that quite a number of things can result in intelligence failing to reach its genetic potential, and that while most intelligent people have intelligent children and dull people dull children, this is no general rule. We have better evidence about what retards intelligence than what enhances it, just because it seems likely that we have an inherent upper limit

[16] While some forms of mental deficiency are heritable, far more of the worst cases are due to damage or disease, either before or after birth. Since brain tissue cannot regenerate, people in whom it is once damaged will never function to their full genetic potential. Such cases increase the lower end of the I.Q. distribution, but need not alarm the eugenicist.

[17] The test/retest variation is usually 10–20 points, and the different "years" of such tests are known not to be strictly equivalent.

to our potential intelligence, and we reach this in a good environment and fail to do so in a poor one. We also have some evidence that the environment of early childhood is more critical than that of later years. But anything more is really speculation in the present state of knowledge. Alarming questions like "Is national intelligence declining?" are really unanswerable in constantly changing social and educational conditions, and anyway have a sort of spurious quality about them, being more proper to journalism than to science. Mad efforts to improve national intelligence by bribing the bright to breed and sterilizing the mental defective are equally unjustified in the present state of knowledge—they are dictated by feeling rather than reason.

Genius and special abilities of one kind or another have always a special interest and some of the earliest studies attempted to unravel the genetics of these,[18] but it is by no means easy. It does emerge that, while most musical geniuses are the product of families without any others in them, the families of good musicians produce proportionally far more. What we can infer from this is just a shade doubtful; musical families would early recognize ability and provide an environment likely to stimulate and encourage it. The same goes for other forms of talent. We can on this evidence neither rule out the possibility of heredity endowment nor really decide on the extent of its importance.

## The inheritance of temperament

When we come to temperament, although we have less information, what we have is a little less confusing since the animal studies are rather more relevant.

It is quite clear from the start that personality as we see it in the adult is achieved rather than given, but what sort of personality we come to have rests in part on the sort of emotional predispositions with which we come into the world.

[18] Galton, F., *Inquiries into Human Faculty and its Development* (1883).

It has been shown that in animal populations timidity, savageness, aggression and activity have all heritable variations. We can breed selected groups of dogs or rodents in which such temperamental traits differ greatly. Equally we can demonstrate some of the mechanism of inheritance by cross-breeding genetically distinct groups which differ in temperament.[19] While such studies are in their relatively early stages today, they are promising enough to give some support to the age old theories of the poets, philosophers, dramatists, novelists and doctors that we differ in psychological constitution. But exactly how much, and why, is by no means so clear. Also on the face of it such differences are probably of a rather gross and general kind, experience determining how they ultimately manifest themselves in personality. Perhaps the best authenticated temperament trait of this kind is what we might call general activity; babies differ markedly in this. An active child given no opportunity to exercise itself may become either irritable, or relapse into inertia; a passive child given adequate stimulation may be alert although placid—given none at all it may be a real pudding. It also seems highly probable that some people have a much lower threshold for both fear and aggression than others[20]; it will take a lot less to make such children fighting mad than others, but the sort of handling and training a child receives will really decide what sort of person emerges. Since this is so, it follows that absolutely the same treatment of two children who differ in basic temperament will produce very different results. Since, in a free breeding heterozygous population, such as we are, people are quite likely to produce children who differ markedly from themselves in temperament this can

[19] Fuller, J. L., and Thompson, W. R., *Behaviour Genetics*, Wiley, New York (1960).

[20] Scott, J. P., *Aggression*, Univ. of Chicago Press, Chicago (1958). In this book Scott gives an account of some of his work on these traits in dogs and rodents, which are probably the most complete studies yet made; the book is quite intelligible to the general reader and worth attention. His comments on human psychology are, however, somewhat less interesting.

make for considerable difficulty and bewilderment. Active people who produce quiet, placid children may provoke them into sulky indifference. Quiet, passive people may be quite unable to handle a very active child. But taking it by and large such variations are usually accepted fairly philosophically and people learn as they go along how to get on with their young; but the failures can be tragic.

If we allow that such variations in temperament occur it can be seen how populations may come in time to differ somewhat in temperament. Because certain types are admired they will be selected for in one way or another. It seems unlikely that genetic distinctions, unless extreme, are as important as learned patterns of behaviour, but some selection may occur. In controlled populations such selection is much more likely, for example, in animals kept for domestic purposes, sometimes in slave populations. But this is rather beyond what we are normally interested in. Whatever the evidence for heredity determinants of behaviour, one thing is abundantly clear: experience is critical in deciding what the end product is like. What we may learn from a study of such temperamental differences is what sort of problems different people are faced with and how they can best cope with them. It should also cause us to pause in lightly giving moral overtones to characteristics which we think of as undesirable. Innate temperamental characteristics are neither meritorious nor otherwise; it may be a misfortune to a child to be aggressive or passive but hardly its fault.

## SOME DOUBTFUL HYPOTHESES

### The inheritance of virtues and vices

It has been argued by some extreme exponents of psychoanalysis that such highly differentiated emotions as envy and gratitude can be inborn in varying quantities. Freud, in a bad moment, made a similar suggestion about selfishness; but Bowlby kindly, and I think correctly, attributes this to a lack of knowledge of both young children and of genetics, adding that Freud realized the need for more information on both topics which was simply not available at the time.

Melanie Klein[21] on the other hand develops a theory in which this is a critical hypothesis and not a passing aside. The idea that such traits could be quantitatively inherited seems, on the face of it, so improbable that one is tempted to dismiss the whole notion out of hand. This may be too slick in view of the extent to which such works are read by people who have insufficient knowledge to examine them critically.

Melanie Klein argues that the phantasy life of infants is extremely complex and that from birth they are more or less prone to envy. Now to postulate "envy" in a baby less than six months old is to argue that it can clearly comprehend a something to be envious of, that it has a notion of self which is clear enough to contrast its present state with the enviable state. Gratitude is just a little easier because it is less complex intellectually, though it still involves the identification of the gift or service with the giver who is experienced as distinct from the self. To argue that a baby is not only envious but innately more or less so is, then, to postulate in that baby not only a precise quantity of emotion of a highly differentiated kind but also a complex intellectual function. It could well be that the argument could be restated in some less dubious form, particularly if one replaced the word "envy" by "jealousy", but of course that would change the theory.

People are capable of jealousy and gratitude quite early in life; at least in later babyhood you can describe their behaviour in these terms just as you can that of a dog or a monkey. It may be that with some sorts of temperament interacting with some sorts of environment either attitude will early come to predominate, but there seems little or no justification for arguing a quantitative inheritance for either trait. With all such arguments as these (and there are many semi-popular

[21] Klein, M., *Envy and Gratitude*, Tavistock Publications, London (1957).

versions of the same thing) it is usual for the evidence on which the statements are based to be very remote from the postulated origin. This often means that the author is relatively unfamiliar with genetic theory and the remotely possible mechanisms for such a state of affairs.

It is quite impossible to identify either envy or gratitude, pride or lust, or any such thing in a baby under six months old; as we have already seen it is difficult enough to identify pleasure or pain, rage, fear and joy. These emotions require language for their explicit expression and final differentiation into complex emotions. Once we get back past the language barrier into the prelinguistic stages of life, we have only behaviour and inference to go on, and all recollections of those months recalled in language will be tinged with the sophistication of language itself. I am not suggesting that we can formulate no ideas about these early years or months, but only that we should be both cautious and economical in formulating hypotheses about the genesis and nature of psychological events within them. There is no particular reason why, once there is any sign of memory, a baby should not have an imaginative life—indeed there is very good reason for supposing it does. Equally there are good reasons for judging that its interest focuses very much on itself, its body processes and people on whom it is dependent for psychological and physical care. Many of the psychoanalytic hypotheses about infancy are for this reason highly plausible, if capable of only indirect verification. It is, for example, much more probable that infants have some sort of phantasy life comparable to that of children and adults than that they are totally devoid of this and acquire it quite suddenly with speech. Any system of psychology which ignores this aspect of human behaviour and experience (as does that of many of the more strict behaviourists) is bound to be limited and inadequate.

The differential inheritance of the virtues and vices which characterize adult life seems to be a hypothesis which, however much it attracts or repels, is not only "wild" but scarcely capable of verification. We are all probably born with a potential capacity for envy and gratitude, for selfishness or altruism; but these are names we give to people's actions when we are capable of the moral evaluation they inevitably imply—without that evaluation they would have other names.

## The inheritance of phantasy

A very different problem is raised by Jung's theory of the collective unconscious, a theory of hereditary phantasy. These are two rather separate questions, and the theory is discussed here only because it seems to involve the inheritance of acquired characteristics. As far as the more general theory goes it would have belonged more properly in the previous chapter, but this aspect of differential inheritance requires attention, and Jung's theory provides a good context in which to discuss it.

Jung's own writing is rich, diffuse and poetic—with the result that any attempt to summarize his theories or views usually distorts them and robs them of a good deal of their value and interest. Nevertheless, some of the hypotheses he put forward are so central to his writing that they may be extrapolated with reasonable safety. He suggests that each individual inherits a "collective unconscious" which is a common property of the human psyche; that this unconscious contains images and phantasies which each individual shares with all others—some of these common phantasy patterns or figures he calls archetypes.[22] In addition, the individual has racial and familial aspects to his unconscious—also inherited—and finally a sort of personal deposit of phantasies and memory which is his alone. This is a very summary account and may be unfair. It also ignores a notion, which personally I find extremely hard to understand and even harder to believe, that the "group mind" has a quasi-substantial existence outside the individuals

[22] Sometimes he suggests that archetypes are really "modes" not images, and the psychological equivalent of instincts. But the argument supposes a heritable quality to such psychic contents. Jung says they are "inherited with the brain structure".

who comprise the group. But to keep to the aspect of the idea which seems capable of examination, this contains two separate postulates, first that we inherit the disposition to form archetypical images, and these are in an active focii of psychic energy, and secondly that in racial memory acquired characteristics are heritable.

I will deal with the second of these ideas first. Repeated attempts to demonstrate that the inheritance of characteristics acquired during the life time of an animal or plant can be passed on to their offspring have on the whole been resoundingly unsuccessful. While some biologists still hold the so called "Lamarckian" hypothesis, the weight of opinion is against it. So that for physical characteristics of animals and plants such an hypothesis is barely tenable.[23] For psychological characteristics the only possible evidence for such a theory derives from one of McDougall's experiments[24]; this experiment was successful but numerous attempts to repeat it have always produced negative results. The chances are that if such a process can occur it does so very rarely and is an incredibly difficult thing to bring about; the probability that it is a common occurrence or a usual means of passing on characteristics is remarkably small. Further, in animal and plant species such a process would be at a biological premium; evolution through selection among random variations is a very slow process and a wasteful one.

In man the pressures which bring about evolution in animal species are at a minimum, since social transmission is possible through speech, and skills and information can be amassed so quickly through successive generations that the need for slower processes of bodily evolution is not very great. In addition, we use much of our learning and skill to offset those biological pressures which would ruthlessly select among our members. If McDougall's results are taken at their face value, it took fourteen generations to get a population of rats which

[23] There is some evidence for such an effect but it is very slight.
[24] McDougall, W., "Second report on a Lamarckian Experiment", *Brit. J. Psychol.* (1930), **20**, 201–18.

took the correct turning in a maze offering a choice of left and right; you can get the same effect in a human population thousands strong by putting up a notice saying "Turn left" (in both cases a few poor things will always turn right). This all suggests that Jung's genetic theory has a very tenuous claim to our attention.

But to return to the first, and more important idea, that we share a common inheritance of phantasy images, this deserves greater attention. It can mean either that each of us arrives in the world with such phantasies latent within us[25] or that we are so organized that once phantasy becomes a possibility it will have certain common features—certain ideas and images will have greater attraction than others, be more vivid, more meaningful. It would be a delicate and difficult task to decide whether natural bent of mind or cultural diffusion gives us the more probable explanation for this, but it is likely to be both. Since there is an apparent limit to the stories we can make up, at least in terms of basic plot, the same ideas and themes are bound to recur, but there still seems to be something in the idea that some images are more compelling than others. We pick such ideas from our cultural heritage and endow them with personal significance. Thus our phantasy will have common elements and unique elements. Further we have the undoubted fact that human life confronts all of us with certain similar and central experiences, with conflicts and problems which find an echo in nearly every human life.

The great creative writers survive from age to age just because they treat of such central themes, which survive the particulars of time and place and, in the hands of a great writer, speak to the essential human condition. These experiences and problems arise because we are made and grow in such a way that they are inevitable; what we make of them varies from person to person and from culture to culture from age to age. That some of these things should be reflected in common

[25] Jung states it in this way sometimes but does not maintain this view at all consistently.

phantasies is perhaps remarkable, because such phantasies seem freer of the particulars of day to day existence than most of our thoughts or ideas, but they hardly justify a mystique. What we may need to postulate to account for such "archetypical" phenomena is not really a principle of racial memory, or group mind, but either a certain preconditioning of our thought processes (whereby certain images distil from experience and so provide a symbolic imaginative synthesis of the essential elements in experience), or a process like that already described in the discussion of IRM's[26] (a process latent in the organism, which is brought to life by experience and fixed by it). These images could then be said to await experience, and perhaps need very little of it to establish the fitness of the image. I think it is probable that we may in fact need both of these ideas, or one which will in some way combine them. Faced with an archetypical image, the person may experience a sense of its attraction or "fitness", may be able to make immense use of it in the never ceasing process of organizing experience into a meaningful whole.

In general it would be true to say that in thinking and imagination we have an orientation which to some extent dictates both the way in which we set about these things and their content. Language is a tool we learn to think with, particularly to think abstractly, and at the same time moulds and limits the way in which we do so. So that language is stereotyped, limiting and artificial, yet it is the characteristic form for new and original thinking. In phantasy and imagination we deal in a large part with common experience, shared legends, stories, symbols, which give us the most vital expression of our own inner and unique life and experience. It is this paradox which makes the controversies about the innate and acquired so meaningless.

[26] Cf. Chapter 1.

# CHAPTER IV

# THE GROWTH OF
# INDIVIDUALITY

## BEGINNINGS

### The individual

The individual who inherits both general and particular characteristics and who is born into, and deeply involved in, society, although he is largely shaped by this heritage, is no less distinct as a person because of this. We derive some measure of our uniqueness from the minor variations in heredity which we have already discussed, and from differences in our experience which are inevitable; and we derive our intelligibility from our social environment. Nevertheless in life in society we are profoundly interested in, and concerned with, our individuality; few people believe themselves to be other than fascinating (with a certain justification), and those few who never interest anyone, not even themselves, are part of the tragedy we call "abnormality". The value which we place on the individual in our civilization is probably a legacy of our Christian culture, but one which we would be reluctant to lose. However unsuccessful we may be in allowing the individual to develop to his full maturity, we at least pay lip service to the propriety of such an aim.

When we see people in everyday life we see actions, purposes and apparent intentions. We see X working, very concerned about his status relative to Y, anxious to make money, fond of his wife who irritates him, thinking about his ulcer, wondering about a nuclear holocaust, and buying a gramophone record to, as he puts it, "take his mind off things". In addition, he may be and do a whole host of other things, but we shall be able to discern a pattern in his preoccupations and interests, which gives him a consistency which we call his personality.

But to understand personality we need to understand the structures which are the bones of this existential reality, the interests, attitudes and sentiments which make personality in this sense possible. Within the limited compass of this book it is plainly impossible to consider every aspect of human personality, selection is inevitable; so that in the account which follows I shall concentrate on those aspects of personality which are particularly concerned with the interests and values of the individual because these are most critical to an understanding of self-determination.

### Living in a family

In the normal course of events a baby starts life in a family of some sort. The precise form of the family can vary greatly, particularly in the size of group involved. In some societies the parents and child are virtually merged in a much wider group consisting of grandparents, aunts, uncles, cousins and so on; in others they are virtually isolated. Institutional as opposed to family rearing is rare except in complex societies, and even in these the basic family unit tends to persist even under strong political pressure to suppress it.

Children who have no surviving parents, or parents who for one reason or another desert them, are in most societies reared by other relatives if they survive at all. The growth of institutions to care for children in such unfortunate circumstances is probably peculiar to our own civilization, and arose in the first place as a charitable effort to keep alive and care for abandoned children. The idea that such institutional care was better for the child in some way has from time to time gripped the imagination of the social planner, but, since children fail to thrive in ideal institutions and people usually dislike having their children reft from them, it has never been widely adopted.[1]

What all young children seem to need is some person to whom they can form an attachment; such a person must recur in the child's life at fairly frequent intervals to supply this need; the child may be able to cope with two or three people, but more than that allows him to form no consistent relationship. Further, he needs more than just washing and feeding; he needs a minimum of handling, to be nursed, played with or generally jostled. Too much attention may make him irritable and over-excited, but some he must have. When he gets older he needs to be talked to, or at least talked around, if he is not going to become retarded in his own speech development. In ordinary family life such requirements are easily met—if you are bathing one baby it seems natural to talk to it and play with it; if you are bathing ten it is easier just to get on and wash them as fast as possible. You do not have to make an effort to expose a baby to the spoken word in any ordinary family; but if you have two hundred separated into age groups,

[1] Within the charitable structure itself it has been increasingly realized that the large hygienic institution full of highly qualified staff does not seem either physically or psychologically well adapted to the child's needs—infant mortality rates are apt to be high. That is not to say that the worst family is better than a good institution, but rather that successful institutions are those which are small and most closely resemble a family in structure. It is widely recognized today that good foster homes provide a better solution to the problems raised by unprovided-for children; but, failing this, the grouping of children of both sexes and mixed ages into small homes with a house mother and father is a considerable improvement on the monolithic single-sex institution run by a necessarily remote matron or superintendent with constant changes of nurses and other workers. We can judge this pattern to be the best since it produces the healthiest and best-adapted children. It must be remembered that a good institution of reasonable size, in the charge of the right person, is a lot better than a succession of inadequate, indifferent foster parents. The other thing to remember is that children with special problems may require unusual treatment and care, which may be better provided in some kind of institution.

it becomes more likely that the amount of talk the child hears is limited.[2]

It would appear that in order to become an adequate human being you require someone from whom to learn; the natural sequence is that you learn about your mother and then your immediate family and gradually extend your range to the world at large.[3] Deprived of this opportunity the child may lack any real capacity for affection, for any real warmth of feeling towards others. Love is most easily learnt from the experience of being loved and from the security which such love provides. Without a capacity for love a person is psychologically crippled, and for the baby the experience of love seems to consist in being cared for physically, being talked to and played with and perhaps in simply having someone there when he needs this.

*Priority in time*

Of course people differ very greatly in their capacity to meet these demands of infancy, and negative patterns set up by failures in this early relationship may persist into later life. It may seem that I am labouring this point, but in order to understand the later attitudes of the individual it is vital to see how their emotional tone may derive from what are, chronologically speaking, very primitive experiences. These will account not so much for the precise content of preferences and values, but the type of satisfaction the individual is seeking, the sort of thing he is prepared to attempt, and the directions in which his energy is expended.

At the beginning of independent life the infant's interests and wants are limited and immediate. It takes many months for even a rudimentary sense of time to develop, and much longer for any clear sense of a precise location of events in time to

[2] Goldfarb, "The effect of early institutional care on adolescent personality", *J. Exper. Educ.* (1943), **12**, 106–29.

[3] Suttie, I., in *The Origins of Love and Hate*, Kegan, Trench & Trubner, London (1935), describes this process most vividly.

be apparent. A two-year-old will appreciate the meaning of "not now", and some sequence of past events, but his idea of the future is dim in the extreme; tomorrow is an unknown quantity as remote as next year. This gives a peculiar quality to early experiences and may have a lot to do with their intensity and importance. The philosophical reflection that "all things pass" is one of maturity, one that, in his way, the adolescent is quite as unable to grasp as the baby. Because the immature are vulnerable to experience, have a limited capacity to envisage a future beyond the present in any realistic terms, they are much more readily moulded by experience; were they not so, they probably would not learn so much or so fast as they do. This gives a certain irreversibility to their learning, which is really what we mean by saying that the experiences of early life determine in a large measure what the individual will be like.

Experience is the raw material out of which we build our attitudes, expectancies and habits of life; early experiences become the reference point for dealing with later experiences and will colour their meaning. Since the individual constantly interprets experience, once a bias is set up it tends in some measure to be self-perpetuating. In very simple terms this means that someone who has experienced rejection and hostility will come to expect such reactions, and hence may well be able to interpret enough of his experiences in these terms to confirm his expectancy a large part of the time. Such circles of expectations are not unbreakable but are very resistant, which is one of the reasons why most forms of psychotherapy require very considerable time and effort on the part of both the patient and the therapist.

## INTERESTS

### Early interests

One consequence of the intense early attachment of the infant to its mother and its involvement in family relationships is that he picks up many of the habits and values of that family and so, in the way that has already been suggested in Chapter II, acquires his culture. But, even while he is thus engaged, evolving individual patterns of interest and ways of behaviour begin to be formed. Some of these early interests fade with growing maturity, others persist in some form. Children for example vary greatly in how much they respond to music, or the extent to which they gain satisfaction in painting or modelling, but they nearly all gain some satisfaction in these pursuits. Whether such interests persist depends a good deal on aptitude, but opportunity and encouragement seem more critical in the early years. A child under five is so susceptible to the selective pressures of his environment that his interests have only a limited autonomy. Of course it is often the strength of the reaction that the child responds to rather than the direction; an interest may be maintained by opposition strong enough to focus attention on the child, and extreme encouragement may kill an interest off as easily as extreme disapprobation. The sort of encouragement which constantly draws the child's attention to his inadequacy will discourage what it is meant to cultivate; children do not like people breathing heavily down the backs of their necks, telling them how to do it better, although they usually put up with it more gracefully than adults.

## Reversals and changes

Because of their intense dependence, their need for approval and their limited capacity for self control, children may show a form of reversal in a strongly disapproved interest which is sometimes called a *reaction formation*: a discouraged enjoyment of playing with dirt (or substances so defined by adults) may lead a child to become so intensely clean and tidy as to daunt his mentors considerably. Such reversals are relatively uncommon in adults though occasionally seen in brain-washed individuals and in certain types of "conversion" in which the individual becomes a sort of negative print of his previous self.

This kind of reversal is characteristic of the unconscious modification of interest and must be carefully distinguished from a more rational process which can lead, by a comparatively leisurely route, to the reversal of previously held opinion. It is also perhaps worth adding, in view of some of the recent writing on the subject,[4] that such reaction formation is not at all the same as the effect of sudden insight which may also give rise to "conversion". Which process one is dealing with can only be seen by a careful analysis of the person and situation involved. An example of the latter of a very simple kind is the change which may be observed in some people's attitude towards fur coats when they have been given a sufficiently graphic account of the way in which the furs are obtained. Some people may remain indifferent but others may find that, unless they can assure themselves that the one time owners of the pelts met their end in some relatively "humane" way, their interest in fur coats has taken a steep downward turn and their behaviour may be modified accordingly. One value system is here seen, through additional information, to exert a determining influence upon another. The same sort of modification of behaviour may be seen in attitudes towards people when some unexpected insight is gained into their behaviour; one may come to love people one initially disliked intensely and of course vice versa. Whether such changes of feeling are rational or otherwise is often obvious to the observer if not to the people involved; they will in any case always have a logic of some kind but it may be an unconscious one.

This is a digression, but not entirely irrelevant because changes of opinions and interests are important. They are characteristic in some measure of the process of maturing; typically they slow down markedly in adult life. Among those who remain chronically immature interests may change more readily, but these are often very superficial; typically such

[4] Notably, Sargent, W., in *Battle for the Mind*, Heinemann, London (1957).

people's response is, like that of the young child, to the social effect of the interest rather than to the thing in itself. To do what other people are doing, or not doing, to collect what they collect, to be the same, to be different, to go one better than the other person, all matter more than whatever particular thing is involved. Such elements of course persist in all shared concerns, but while in some cases people who share an interest come together, in other cases people who come together share an interest; an exclusive adherence to either pattern is in some measure unsatisfactory, the one involving an egotistical refusal to consider other people unless they fit in with you, and the other a frame of mind acceptable in an eight-year-old but sacrificing any proper independence of mind in an adult.

## Interests and values

We give our attention to things that interest us, and in so doing we learn more about them, we may become sufficiently absorbed to become involved in other types of learning and activity which have some relevance to the original interest. In this way we build up specialized knowledge and skills and develop our judgement. It has been argued by some people that the original "motive" in an interest remains its major dynamism; but others[5] maintain that an interest once established becomes functionally autonomous and thus, independent of its origins, provides its own motivation. Both points of view have something to be said for them. Some interests seem clearly over-determined; they can be seen to satisfy needs beyond their apparent scope. Still others are largely accidental, brought about by exposure, so to speak, in the pursuit of some more important goal; these may or may not persist, they may become autonomous if they are found to satisfy in themselves. Many people know the experience of taking a mild interest in something to please someone else and finding in the end that it has become more important to them than the person

[5] Cf. Allport, G. W., *Personality*, Holt, New York (1937).

ever was.[6] When such interests take hold they usually fit, that is, they satisfy the person in some way. A tone-deaf person is unlikely to develop any real passion for music, but to a person with a natural feeling for music casual exposure to it may provide the beginning of an absorbing interest.

In some measure "sublimation" enters into the picture; this is a difficult idea but an important one. Even if one rejects most of the psychoanalytic theory of instinctual energy, the principle that the same emotional impulse may find expression in ways which are useful and socially acceptable or otherwise may be found valid. The fact that chopping wood may at times make an acceptable way of discharging aggression does not mean that it is the only reason for doing it, nor that it is not useful in this way from time to time. This is the sort of example which puts the process at its simplest and crudest. The human mind can be relied upon to elaborate any useful process of this kind to a very great level of complexity.

I have perhaps made the interests sound a bit remote and more like hobbies, or those things which people frantically think up to fill in the dreary blank spaces on forms which demand information of this kind. The aspiring university student fills such blanks with things like football, photography and dramatics, because he is expected to; the fact is that his real interests in life are things like getting into a university, mathematics, making money, meeting new people and so on. But this simply reflects the peculiarities of language and social custom. A person's long-term goals are the measure of his interests and the energy he expends upon them a fair measure of their importance to him.[7] The principle of hierarchy is once again at work and some of these goals and interests will be

[6] Or equally for one reason or another we are forced to pay attention to something we find dull or difficult, perhaps in pursuit of another goal, perhaps because we have no choice, and find in the end we are interested after all. The pious hope of many educators is that if they force little Willy to learn Greek he will love it in the end.

[7] Allport, G. W., *Pattern and Growth in Personality*, Holt, New York (1961).

much more critical than others. Those to which the individual is most deeply committed may be so much himself and his way of life that he can scarcely think of himself apart from them; he thinks of himself as, say, a scientist with an interest in protozoa who likes occasionally to play the clarinet rather than as interested in science, protozoa and the clarinet in that order.

Spranger[8] suggested that we could classify people in terms of their dominant value system of which he suggested six as basic types: theoretical, economic, social, aesthetic, political and religious. Without going into this in any detail, it is worth saying that such values are reflected in "interest" (willingness to pay attention to things relevant to the value dimension), knowledge, often size of specialized vocabulary, and the distribution of the individual's time and energy.

## Boredom

It is possible for someone to be so limited that you could hardly say they had any real interests or goals at all, but even such people make visible if minimal efforts to keep boredom at bay. They do this largely through a system of passive attention; the storyteller in all forms is a valuable member of society because he entertains without demanding too much. There are other devices; high among them one can put gossip and speculation about people's doings and motives, things like gambling and various forms of games. Some of these attract people because they involve a certain amount of intellectual effort, and for the more intelligent person this is rewarding, but the moment the person becomes more than minimally involved physically or intellectually he ceases to be passive. The attraction of what might be called intellectual thumb-twiddling is considerable, and it seems to give satisfaction on two counts, one because it is satisfactory to use one's intelligence and secondly because it provides a potential source of achievement —crossword puzzles, number games, even things like chess

[8] Spranger, E., *Types of Men*, Niemeyer, Halle (1928).

give this sort of satisfaction to the right people. But they remain self-limiting devices however absorbing; they are an active form of rest. From all of this we can infer that the mind abhors a vacuum, the person prefers to be occupied however trivially, though for most people passive space filling is not a way of life but an aspect of it. In a society like our own, in which leisure is becoming increasingly common, this is an aspect of life which demands attention; some people are concerned with the quality of the bread and circuses which leisure will demand.

## SENTIMENTS

### Formation and function

To return once more to childhood. One of the major systems which controls our interests and sets of values is the growth of widening emotional attitudes which are usually called sentiments. These we form in relation to people, objects and ideas; they form a large part of what might be called our emotional ballast, the stable and predictable elements of our character. Such sentiments differ in importance, they exhibit in fact some species of hierarchy. The simplest of these sentiments may be virtually wordless, but even the toddler's attachment to his teddy bear does not remain wordless for long, and in the more typical case long-term memory and a complex use of language seem to keep the structure of any sentiment system tight. Some sentiments are of so abstract a kind that language seems essential to their formation and certainly to their persistence. This does not mean that anyone can turn round and give a slick and full account of his sentiments at the drop of a hat, but, among other things, that such sentiments are most easily studied in linguistic terms. Word association techniques, the use of scales which allow the individual to select adjectives that he considers appropriate to certain objects, people and ideas,[9] statements

[9] Osgood, C. E., *The Measurement of Meaning*, Univ. of Illinois Press, Urbana (1957), describes one of the most efficient of these techniques, known as the "semantic differential".

with which a person can agree or disagree, all prove effective means of giving objective information about the things he loves, hates, values, derides, etc. These enduring emotional dispositions have been described in various ways and some people dislike the word sentiment in this context, preferring a notion like channelling of emotion,[10] but some concept of the kind must be employed for any adequate description of the person's affective life.

Sentiments can be mixed in emotional tone[11]—typically a love/hate balance that we call ambivalence, but other oppositions are possible. In such states of ambivalence it is usual for one aspect to be much more clearly recognized than the other. In some cases either aspect may be deeply repressed, but it will manifest itself in a number of ways behavioural and verbal.[12] In the sentiment system we find the clue to what appeals to the individual, what repels him and that to which he is indifferent.

The experience of actual emotion will be largely in terms of these systems once they are established, and rather more rarely in what might be called essentially immediate terms. For example, the great British public experiences a wave of indignation when someone treads on a dog's tail on purpose and they hear about it; of course, they are also indignant if someone treads on their own toe; valued people, objects, classes of objects and ideas account for a good deal of human reactivity.[13] In Sherif and Cantril's term where we have strong

[10] Cf. Murphy, G., *Human Potentialities*, Basic Books, New York (1958).

[11] The strength of the persistent emotional interest, among other things, advertises the sentiment rather than the type of emotion.

[12] Slips of the tongue and pen, dreams and word associations all give verbal clues to the repressed, and a variety of "accidents" may give behavioural evidence of the unacknowledged aspect of the sentiment.

[13] Philips, M., *The Education of the Emotions*, Allen & Unwin, London (1937), suggests that in very immature individuals only the "self-sentiment" is at all well developed; such people are characterized by a lack of any real emotional investment in anyone or anything beyond themselves, that is, they attach importance to other people and

sentiments we are "ego-involved": the objects of our attachment become a part of ourselves.

More peripheral to our personality are what are usually called attitudes, this means what we think of this and that; the word attitude here has a value in that it deals with ideas of a sort which may reflect our sentiment systems, but are more properly the verbal expression of our views coloured by our sentiments, reflecting information, prejudices and derivative thinking. We may have, for example, an attitude towards war, coloured by our sentiments about Napoleon, our personal hostility, the current political situation, our religious beliefs and so on. As Gallup polls frequently demonstrate, attitudes change; sentiments are tougher on the whole.

## Coherence in personality

The basic structure of the personality is provided by the individual's primitive need system and the degree of satisfaction which he has enjoyed and the way in which it has been experienced. This system itself is only broadly defined and becomes particular through extensive learning. Beyond this, a complex sentiment structure becomes the semi-permanent focus of his values and interests.

In the structure of personality it is possible to distinguish both conscious and unconscious elements. Part of the unconscious processes are concerned with control of behaviour through mechanisms of guilt, part with impulses to action of one kind or another and part with memory of experiences and events. Past impulses which are not readily available to conscious introspection may at times exert considerable controlling influence in the individual's life, being experienced in consciousness both as impulse and emotion but without cognizance of their precise origin. The more conscious aspects of the

---

things only in terms of their direct effect upon themselves—in this example they would be more concerned with their own toe than the dog's tail!

personality (or "ego" processes) are more concerned with the appraisal of reality as it is currently experienced, with thinking, with choice and with the practical realities of living. So strong is the overmastering drive towards meaning that when un-recognized emotions and desires obtrude into consciousness these are nearly always "explained" in some way that is con-gruent with consciously accepted attitudes. These processes I have already described as ego-defence mechanisms. The impor-tant thing to note here is that they are incidental to the most important aspect of ego functioning which is the constant pro-cess or organization towards coherence. Sometimes such co-herence is bought at the price of distorting the reality currently experienced, because the congruence thus achieved is the only one which allows the individual's picture of himself to remain intact.

## The self-knowledge

The individual's view of himself which we could call his conscious self-knowledge is central to the whole personality. It is an idea which, under several different names, is an important aspect of ego psychology in any system. Most authors place its beginnings in the second year of life. Sullivan[14] argued most cogently for the critical rôle of language in the formula-tion of what he called the self dynamism, language being, he argued, essential to the exclusion of certain aspects of the real self from this perceived and accepted self. The very crude workings of such a process can be seen in most young children; it is often considered as mere lying by adults, but the child who announces after a loud crash, "It wasn't me that broke the teapot which has just smashed itself", is also involved in the process of defining himself as an "un-teapot-smashing" person. This self image has a dual aspect: a "me as I am" and a "me as I'd like to be" (variously called the ego ideal, idealized self image and so on), both of which differ in some

[14] Sullivan, H. S., *The Interpersonal Theory of Psychiatry*, Norton, New York (1953).

measure from the totality, that is, the whole person. In most neurotic conditions both the self-image and the ideal self are badly distorted and more than usually incongruent with one another[15] but, neurosis apart, some people come very much closer to real self knowledge than others. It requires a good deal of security and a high degree of personal integration to achieve such knowledge and yet it would seem to be the proper result of all the conscious tendency to seek sense and meaning in experience. It seems to be generally agreed that there are limits to the actual possibilities for self-knowledge because of real limits to the possibility of verbalizing experience, but the degree of distortion and of discordance may be great or relatively small, and often offers a rough measure of the mental health of the individual or of his maturity. "Know thyself" is necessarily a counsel of perfection, but not a meaningless objective.

## AWARENESS

We have considered those aspects of personality which the individual can do very little to modify; they make him in a large measure what he is and even determine to some extent how far he understands what he is. This framework of personal experience is filled out with a great deal of information of a fairly straightforward kind, with a great complex of skills and abilities; the person's conscious life is filled with interests, feelings, and the constant play of intelligence upon immediate experience, and the relevant memories which this evokes. Much of this field of experience is not in the forefront of awareness —there is a vast hinterland of ideas, memories, perceptions, knowledge, which can become itself the focus of attention as the situation demands. An array of vigilance systems seems constantly to scan the periphery of sensory experience, keeping the individual orientated in time and space, and keeping out of the field of direct awareness material which is low in interest

[15] Rogers, C. and Dymond, R., *Psychotherapy and Personality Change*, Univ. of Chicago Press, Chicago (1954).

value and would "interrupt" what is going on there. But even in sleep this outer attention system continues its task, allowing us to sleep through some things and to wake in the presence of others. The sound of a person's name will, for example, catch his attention and wake him from a light sleep,[16] while the sound of someone else's name may not in the formal sense be heard at all in similar circumstances. Unless the person is deeply unconscious (when, for example, he is heavily drugged or has been hit on the head) the whole system continues its organizing programme.

More than just the stimuli from without are involved, the inner processes of phantasy and imagination seem also to be in almost ceaseless activity in the fringes of consciousness. Once again, when this material gets out of hand or assumes threatening aspects it becomes the focus of conscious attention. As Freud has so brilliantly shown,[17] when dreaming becomes a threat to inner stability the person wakes up; most people know the experience of fighting their way to consciousness through the remnants of a nightmare. In the same way, the conscious relaxed person may experience day dreams and phantasies which he may seem to experience rather than contrive, but which he may stop, at least temporarily, if they offend in some way, or an awareness of other demands intrudes.

In all of this we can discern levels of awareness from the narrow field of focused attention, peripheral awareness of the world about us, through the hinterland of ideas working their way tentatively to the surface,[18] the solutions to problems the formulations of new ones, down into more remotely available material which we may call to mind if we need it, and finally to a depth of unawareness of which we only know the very

[16] Oswald, I., *Sleeping and Waking*, Elsevier, Amsterdam (1962).

[17] *The Interpretation of Dreams*, first published 1900, standard edition 1953, Hogarth, London.

[18] Harding, D. W., "The Hinterland of Thought", in *Metaphor and Symbol: Proceedings of the twelfth symposium of the Corston Society*, Butterworth, London (1960).

fringes. That active construction goes on at all these levels of consciousness we know from a variety of experiences, records and experiments. The creative writer, for example, may find his ideas coming "fully fledged" into his mind; bright images, lines of verse, even whole poems seem to just occur and though their ultimate provenance in memory may be analysed,[19] the construction itself may take place largely away from the focus of awareness. It is this sort of experience that gives rise to the impression of possession by an idea, which is sometimes virtually personified, as when Goethe talks of his "possessing daemon" who takes over and writes. But unless such ideas do come into the forefront of experience, unless they become the focus of attention, unless they are seen as valuable, then they remain no more than the material for dreams.

From this we can see that at least one function which the focus of conscious awareness has in the internal economy of the individual is that of appraisal. In this aspect of himself the person judges the importance both of his own ideas and impulses, and his perceptions of the world about him. In the normal course of events the judging, deciding, choosing functions of the individual are peculiarly the property of his conscious and attending self. Of course many judgements and choices are made automatically and in the fringes of awareness; the focus of our attention is not always occupied with such processes, but when choices appear to present us with problems we turn our attention to them. In action we select that to which we turn our attention, and engage ourselves to a greater or lesser extent in that activity. Thus concentration, which is a state of prolonged attention, demands a focusing of ourselves on whatever is to hand. Any baby can concentrate; it is not an esoteric art in spite of what educators may say to the contrary, but many people do very little of it in later life, or at any rate never concentrate very deeply. Equally, many people

[19] Cf. Lowes, Livingstone, *The Road to Xanadu*, Constable, London (1927).

resent concentration in others, because it deflects attention away from themselves or excludes them in some way. But that is rather by the way.[20]

In choosing what to do with either our lives or our leisure we both express our personality and form it. The values which we hold will be partly learnt involuntarily, partly taught deliberately, and partly acquired by ourselves in the continuous process of selection which is living, and it is with this question of choice that I will concern myself in the next chapter.

[20] The ability to use the unconscious self and the margins of awareness in a constructive way, as part of the creative self and not alien to it, is one of the things which may be crippled by an over emphasis on the practical, rational and effortful. A deep mistrust of the intuitive is probably a legacy of nineteenth-century rationalism we could do without.

# CHAPTER V

# THE INDIVIDUAL IN
# ACTION

## *SELECTIVE BEHAVIOUR*

### Minimal conditions

Some form of selective behaviour is demanded by life, however limited the range of opportunities some lives may offer. Where there is little or no choice of foodstuffs, where patterns of work and life are circumscribed and entertainment limited, then the bare struggle for survival will be overwhelming; but even in marginal communities, living on the edge of subsistence, skills are developed that involve complex decisions on the outcome of which life may well depend. The variety of experiences may be severely curtailed by such extreme duress, and the fields in which choice is possible few, but even in such circumstances people vary, and part of that variation derives from different decisions about what matters most, or what is the best approach to some problem.

In other societies custom may dictate the course of a person's actions so clearly that he scarcely feels called upon to make any decisions for himself; he relies on precedent. Accident of birth may fix both his social rôle and his occupation, but it can hardly fix it so completely that he never has to make any choices at all. It is in fact hard to imagine a life in which the person is totally passive, limited on all sides by necessity, though some people may seem to come very close to this condition. It will not be a state in which culture flourishes, it is too nearly a subhuman condition, though slavery, extreme oppression and the condition of women in some primitive societies[1] may provide us with occasional examples. But wherever life offers something very slightly more, then people are faced with choices of one type or another.

### Learning to choose

In the early years of life such selection may seem arbitrary and determined by a few very simple systems of preference. There is a sense in which the baby who spits out a lovely new patent baby food could be said to choose, to act selectively; but if we assume either that the food tastes nasty, or the baby is upset by its novelty, we shall not have to go much further to explain the factors which determine its selective behaviour. Such simplicity is soon lost. A baby may have marked preferences in people, in tastes, in sounds and sights, although these are more usually classifiable as reactions involving preferences than as choice in any formal sense. With greater mobility, and still more with the acquisition of language, the baby becomes able to select for itself to some extent rather than pass judgement on what is offered. But choices are still very difficult when they involve something more than response to present stimuli; this is partly because preference systems are scarcely formalized, partly because the child is not yet able to hold more than one possibility in mind, and partly because he has little capacity to predict either about himself or anything else.

Selective behaviour typically involves all of these processes and they take time to mature since they all require experience. A young child in a toy shop wants everything he sees or nothing or the proprietor's dog. Offered a "choice", he may grab the nearest or the brightest object, but this is more to

[1] According to Jung (in, for example, *Contributions to Analytical Psychology* (1928)) women scarcely emerge as individuals at all in some societies.

comply with the adult requests to "make up his mind" than because he is exercising any real discrimination. This failure in predictive power is obvious in many situations; you can ask a two- or three-year-old if he wants something, he says "no" firmly but takes it quite readily when you give it to him. This lulls the adult into a sense of false security because the day comes when the child really means it. The child may then move into a phase where he takes a maddeningly long time to make up his mind, so long that someone usually makes it up for him either to his indignation or relief, depending how close he is to being able to cope with the situation. It is perhaps important to distinguish between knowing what you want, or want to do, and choosing between possibilities. The toddler may exhibit extreme persistence in pursuit of a goal but still be incapable of selecting between equally attractive possibilities. I dwell on this somewhat because in a measure this situation persists in the adult in a muted form. There are also many aspects of life in which choice is virtually non-existent, either because the preference is so clear that nothing offers any significant competition, or because habit has made the process so automatic as to be quite unreflecting and even unperceived as a choice. Further, certain important choices may themselves exclude the necessity for a great many further decisions.

## The context of choice

It is necessary to distinguish certain elements which come together in the process of choice. These are value systems, preference systems, discrimination, judgement and prediction. They form together one of the most complex sets of activities which the organism performs and it is impossible to simplify a description of such activity past a certain point. I shall here try to sketch in the main features, but each aspect of the problem would require lengthy treatment to give anything like justice to the amount of relevant psychological work which helps us to understand it.

The discussion of choice which follows may seem a bit static; it is very difficult to analyse the process carefully without somehow detracting from its living, dynamic quality. A person is in a constant state of activity of some sort and both the internal and external environment are seldom the same for long. All choices take place in the context of the experience of the moment, and that experience includes changes in the need state of the person and the quality and opportunities of the environment. The individual apprehension of any situation is coloured by this all the time. Many of the examples in what follows are chosen for the sake of simplicity from rather trivial and peripheral aspects of behaviour and experience, otherwise the amount of detail would obscure the discussion. But in talking, for example, of value, we need to bear in mind the changes within the individual which he experiences from moment to moment: a person who is tired, wet, cold and hungry does not see the world with the same eyes as one who is physically comfortable, but how this state appears to the individual may depend on its psychological context; you can be physically comfortable in some prisons and very uncomfortable pursuing some forms of apparent enjoyment.

Some people have suggested that a self-sentiment[2] would include in a value system some assessment of need state, and this may make a useful way of looking at this currently apprehended state of the organism. The external world also has its irrefutable aspects which are always with us, and these will alter in some degree with our felt wants and needs.

Abstract terms, dissection of processes, and examples selected for their simplicity, take much of the vividness and movement out of a description of something which is an important part of the experience of life. So that we must bear in mind the necessary flow of life within which the processes under discussion occur, in order to arrive at a balanced understanding of them.

[2] See Chapter IV.

## PREFERENCE

### Value systems

Value systems we have already considered to some extent[3] and I shall only add a few points here. While values are roughly hierarchical, changes can take place within the hierarchy, particularly in the young. The judged relevance of value system to situation may determine the apparent hierarchy observable in behaviour. Changes of behaviour may arise when a value system is seen to be relevant where previously it had not been considered (this is one of the ways in which the outcome of a decision may have an important influence on behaviour in a further similar choice situation). Value systems are confirmed in action, which is also the way in which they manifest themselves. Finally the abstract qualities of value systems do not typically pre-date adolescence, since intelligence is relatively concrete in its operations until the last major development of intelligence takes place in adolescence. This intellectual growth makes it possible for the person to reflect directly about values which previously are much more usually just accepted, it enables him to sort out his own criteria of importance, to accept or reject what once seemed fixed if unacceptable.

### Pleasantness and preference

Preference systems, although they shade off into value systems, have more to do with liking; in the adult they are dependent on a vast deal of experience and learning, because adult preferences come about largely through a process of learning based on the qualitative aspects of past experience. Taking it very broadly, what gives pleasure is preferred to what gives pain—though curious anomalies can occur in which this rather obvious state of affairs is reversed. Perhaps rather more interestingly we seem to extend our range of pleasurable

[3] Cf. Chapters I and IV.

experiences by exploring the edge of the pain or displeasure dimension. Experiences balanced on this edge between pleasure and pain may come to be themselves highly prized. The sort of pleasure people get from roller-coasters, from mountain climbing, from fireworks and a host of other things, derives in some measure from the experience of a mild degree of fear or anxiety which gives a certain excitement lacking in more humdrum pursuits. In the same way certain items of diet may initially be experienced as unpleasant in the sense that they are bitter or highly spiced, but when persisted with have a capacity to give pleasure just because they have this stimulating quality of near unpleasantness. Things like beer and olives, for example, are not usually relished much by the young, but come to be rated among the major pleasures by many people who got over the initial phase of finding them merely unpleasant.[4]

In the same way, something that looks initially unpleasant, because it involves effort, can actually give more pleasure than something easy if it can be found rewarding in the end. The challenge may itself stimulate and excite, particularly if it is not too great.

The other effect which complicates a simple preference system is that of boredom or satiation. Chocolate creams may be your favourite form of food, but it is an unusual person who feels quite the same about them after he has just eaten half a pound; after a couple of pounds they may actually seem repulsive rather than attractive. Things differ a lot in the degree to which they produce satiation or boredom. Bread, for example, although perhaps dull if unrelieved by other food, stands up better to repetition than a great many more fancy items of diet of which a little may be quite enough. One of the things which seems to characterize great art and literature is the way in which it stands up to continuous consumption—the trivial grows tedious if we pay enough attention to it, the worthwhile

[4] Moore, H. T., *Pain and Pleasure*, New York (1917).

remains in some curious way fresh and interesting, even if it is harder to appreciate at first.

## General principles

Preference systems relate to all manner of things, but to some extent they generalize, and exhibit in this way some degree of economy by enabling us to assess fresh situations or things in the light of our general patterns of preference. Many theories have been advanced about the number and type of general principles involved, it is certainly large, taken over all, but within a limited range of material may be rather easier to analyse. Among designs, for example, we may have a general preference for those which are representational, symmetrical, and show sharp colour contrasts, or for the abstract, asymmetrical and muted. Such general patterns of preference may even cut across categories of things to give even broader principles, so that we may prefer the simple to the complex or something of that kind. Some degree of specialization will be apparent in fields where our interest is deeply involved; here our patterns of preference will be more specific and exact because our powers of discrimination will be finer and differences in consequence more meaningful.

## DISCRIMINATION

### Observing distinction

The ability to discriminate is important both to preference and judgement and consequently to choice. Early perceptual learning seems to ensure that we make a whole range of normal discrimination both between classes of object and levels of intensity of sensory stimuli; such perceptions are governed by a number of well known laws which, since they hold for most of the higher mammals as well as man, are clearly not dependent upon language. But with the acquisition of language we have the possibility of classifying experience much more closely, and there is some evidence that refinements of perceptual discrimination are both facilitated by language and reflected in it. Those distinctions which are important tend to have larger vocabularies available for them,[5] and when we become interested in new distinctions then language is usually developed in which to speak of them. Thus in people there is a critical interaction between perception and language, vocabulary being rich where fine discriminations are required. There is at least some evidence that a technical vocabulary will make it easier for us to perceive distinctions in unfamiliar fields. Equally, experience which forces fine discriminations upon us may lead us to look for verbal labels for these distinctions. These finer aspects of discrimination depend less on the general laws governing perception, than on individual training and learning which give meaning and importance to subtle differences.

Where such minor variations are important they will override the common elements in perception and dominate the whole; in this way they obey an important perceptual law that all perceptions strive towards meaning. For example, the majority of people looking casually at a genuine and fake antique side by side see them as the "same"; to an expert the minor differences which he is trained to perceive will so dominate his perception that the fake may stand out like a sore thumb.

### The expert

It is usual, though by no means always the case, that a person with such expertise will be able to analyse the features which give rise to his discrimination between two apparently similar objects; sometimes he will just "know" the difference, although introspection may enable him to elaborate. Such elaborations and verbal descriptions may provide a set of rules

[5] This holds both for the culture as a whole, which may have a rich vocabulary in certain directions, and for the individual within that culture, who may himself know and use more of that vocabulary than others, or even add to it.

whereby others can make the same sort of discrimination stage by stage. Often such reports are incomplete. The maker of fake furniture knows these rules, for example, and the more exactly he follows them the better his fake—but he is not always able to exhaust the limits of the perceptual possibilities, or they may be too difficult to reproduce; thus the expert merely has to expand his expertise further to the fringe of the noticeable. In other cases the person without expert knowledge may come to have this through repeated attention to "labelled" phenomena —the student learning to identify microscope slides of tissues and X-ray plates does this by a progressive process of matching with expert judgement, and listening to the expert drawing his attention to salient points which he may at first be quite unable to "see" in any strong sense.

*Familiarity*

A great familiarity with a class of objects may give the same level of discriminatory ability in a less formal way, but only if the individual attends to such objects. To most urban dwellers most sheep look pretty much alike, unless they differ greatly in colour, and usually his vocabulary does not extend beyond sheep, lamb, ewe, ram and possibly mutton. To a person who sees a great many sheep differences are noticeable and recognized; he may add a few more words denoting sub-classifications and be able to identify breeds. To the sheep breeder this level of classification is far too crude; he has to be able to see much smaller differences, to identify strains within breeds, prizewinning animals from run of the mill stock, and will certainly be able to recognize individual animals. Armed with a manual on the subject, the urban gentleman could probably manage a considerable number of the formal classifications, but would have trouble with the subtler ones.

These "rules", usually formulated so that knowledge can be compared and passed on, are a formalization of a process which to be really successful must be in some sense personal and felt. The rules can be misleading if they are a substitute for the real understanding that lies behind most complex discriminations, but they serve a valuable purpose in showing other people something of how the expert arrives at his opinion. You may not know how to date something by the decay level in its radio-active carbon, but the principle sounds convincing because it is open to verification if one took the trouble.

## Confusion

One important aspect of such differences in discriminatory ability is that they may produce situations in which the individual has to make a choice between two or more apparently similar possibilities, which he knows or suspects to differ in some way which could be important to him. In such circumstances he will experience considerable confusion. He will endeavour to make his choice reasonable in some way, convince himself that he sees a difference after all, consult an expert or just anyone else who is around, consult an oracle, produce some elaborate rationalization or, assenting to the real dilemma, he may either refuse to choose at all, or use some acknowledged way of solving such meaningless choices as tossing a coin, choosing the second on the left or something of this kind. The degree of importance he attaches to success will usually determine how much trouble he goes to over this. Much the same process can happen the other way round, when things appear to differ which are actually the same (for example, detergents). The thing to bear in mind is that such failures in discrimination do not give rise directly to conflict but to some degree of bewilderment and confusion.

## JUDGEMENT

### Evaluation

Judgement involves both value and discrimination. Judgement occurs in terms of a value dimension: this is judged better than that, heavier than that, or whatever it is. It is distinguishable from discrimination in that it involves essentially the use of some criterion, some scale[6] of comparison. That is, one must judge in terms of something: a chair differs obviously from a table or one table from another, but to see this implies no sort of judgement of the chair or tables. A single object may be, and often is, simultaneously judged on several scales and always against an implied background of other objects real or imagined. If we say that is a good sculpture, weighing about 2 lbs and worth £500, we judge its weight, worth and merit all at once. There is a difference between the weight and worth judgements and the merit one, because in the first two we refer to a fixed scale although we judge the relevant point on them, while when we say that it is "good" we use a scale of a different kind. The scale involved in the judgement "good" is a rank rather than a measure,[7] that is, one on which we judge things in relation to one another rather than in relation to a fixed set of units. Because rank scales depend on the judgement "this is better than that", we probably agree less completely about their use than about the use of conventional scales like weight and money. The rank scale has no outside point of reference which we accept in advance, there are no fixed and agreed units independent of the particular object judged; consequently, we must talk at a different level, but this difference does not mean that one kind of scale is therefore more real than the other. None of these scales would mean much unless people were using them, but those which can be verified against an agreed standard do differ from those which demand only either a con-

---

[6] Scale is used here as a general term to imply some linear measure or polarity, so that we have a scale of weights for heaviness, a scale of inches or centimetres for length, but we also have scales which are not in terms of units but rather felt degree of congruence with the ends of the scale. Thus healthy and unhealthy might be the ends of such a scale and any person's health could be described as nearer one than the other on a "scale".

[7] A good but difficult discussion of this point can be found in *The Handbook of Experimental Psychology*, (ed.) Stevens, S., Wiley, New York (1951), Ch. 1, page 1. "Mathematics, measurement and psychophysics", by Stevens, S., although he does not make quite the same distinction as I have made here.

currence of opinion or a body of expert opinion. In the latter type of scale evidence and argument are important but numerical scaling is virtually meaningless. Most of the judgements which we consider important will be of this latter kind, such as judgements about goodness, beauty, truth. Nevertheless, when we say that we employ a scale, or a pair of polarized ideas (good-bad, true-false) in such judgements this is not meaningless. The scale is a sort of representation of a range of possibilities, and items are placed relative to one another with differing degrees of refinement depending on their importance and the temperament of the person judging. There are qualitative aspects to such judgements which make them more than merely linear ranks, but make it even harder to convert them to a simple numerical system. There are psychologists who attempt to scale such judgements and these scales are quite usable provided all their limitations are borne in mind and they are not promoted to a sort of pseudo-scientific accuracy.

One of the things which is interesting about such scales is the way in which verbal use may outrun functional use. It can be shown that many judgements which people use are habitually confounded, that is, two sets of words are used for what is one judgement. If people are asked to classify a large number of things or statements on several such scales, it can be shown[8] that some of them are so nearly equivalent that the person can be said to make no real distinction; for example, it was found that there is a "collapse" of the good-bad scale on the success-failure one, in contemporary American studies. In this way it can be seen that value systems and value judgements are internally related and reflect one another. Further, people using an unpractised or unfamiliar scale may overtly or covertly substitute one which is more familiar, more trusted or in some other way more acceptable, a familiar example would be the beautiful-ugly with the expensive-cheap scales.

[8] Osgood, *op. cit.*

*Laws*

It can be shown that the process of judging is itself governed by a number of laws; among the more familiar we have the Weber-Fechner law that the just noticeable differences between two stimuli increase in size geometrically with the intensity of the stimuli.[9] There is a tendency particularly in marginal judgements to agree with any strong suggestion from other people[10] present. There is a strong pull exerted by any sort of marker stimulus, or reference point, given on a scale; this is exerted even when the marker is somewhat (but not grossly) misplaced.[11] There is a whole host of evidence on bogus prestige labels; if you say a poem is by Shakespeare, people tend to judge it better, for example, than if you say it is by John Smith— assuming they are not literary experts. But the use of "clues" of this kind in judgement is so complicated that it would lead us too far afield to go into it further.

*Prediction*

Judgement is important as an aspect of prediction, as well as in its own right, and this itself is often critical in choice. When faced with the possibility of doing something or in some way selecting among alternatives, we usually make some attempt to foresee the consequences of such behaviour. This prediction may be of a very simple kind or it may be very involved, that is, we may try to decide whether the additional cream bun will add noticeably to our weight, or we may try to work out the consequences of sending our child to Eton or the local grammar school. Such predictions will usually be made in the light of some knowledge or information which may, or may not, be correct, but cannot in the nature of things be complete. There is a whole psychology devoted to unravelling

[9] This only works within limits; if the stimuli are below threshold clearly it cannot work and if the stimuli are strong enough to approach the pain threshold it also ceases to operate.

[10] Asch, *Social Psychology*, Prentice Hall, New York (1952).

[11] Johnson, D. M., *The Psychology of Thought and Judgement*, Harper, New York (1955).

the sort, and amount, of evidence we require before we will take a chance and our willingness to guess and so forth. In general the less it matters the more likely we are to "take a chance", but temperament makes a good deal of difference to our willingness to gamble.

Judgement enters this predictive process in two ways, first in deciding which are the relevant factors to take into account and, secondly, in weighing up these effects. We may fail to foresee possible outcomes of our actions for all sorts of reasons: we may be limited in intelligence, we may not understand this particular type of situation, we may simply have no knowledge of some factor in the situation and we may in varying degrees deceive ourselves. We may be quite mistaken in our prediction and our judgement hence almost irrelevant. If we decide to take a short cut which turns out to be longer than the alternative route then we are wrong in a quite straightforward way, but if we thought we would chance passing that car on a blind corner and hit something, then our judgement is wrong in a rather different sense.

We improve our predictive systems by paying attention to our successes and failures and to those of other people, and by employing a variety of devices to cut down or control the chance elements in them. In this way we may reach a level of near certainty about the outcome of certain actions which renders the choices involved virtually automatic; this is the basis of most successful learning. Or we may mechanize the process in some way to cut down the amount of selection and prediction which we have to do ourselves. All sorts of self-regulating machines, automatic steering devices and so on, can be perfectly successful at choosing provided we give them all the necessary information and build them so that they can make use of new information. Most of these cybernetic devices take the pain out of judgement and certainly reduce both time and error in judgement provided you ask them to solve the right sort of problems. Mechanical brains play chess very well, and if you manage to give them sufficient information would certainly do better than people because the game is self-limiting. But it is no good asking a machine silly questions like whether it prefers red or blue, or what will be the effect of being rude to your sister-in-law.

In prediction the person tries to estimate both the outcome of a course of action and the way in which it will affect him, and the degrees of probability involved and at the same time the importance of all of these to him; that is, he relates this back to his value system. He may then for a variety of reasons behave differently from the way he planned, usually because he has failed to take some factor, internal or external, into account. This is why one can really only talk of choices retrospectively, because until the person acts we have no real certainty about what he will do, or be able to do. He may go out all keyed up to commit murder but may be prevented by some accident, or some resistance on the part of the victim, or he may, when it comes to the point, "decide" not to do it. It is possible to follow this chain backwards quite accurately, but the forward prediction is much more precarious so that I shall deal with choice in terms of action rather than intention.

## CHOICE

### Seeing the alternatives

The background to choice can be seen to involve the complex integration of various facets of the personality and can be correctly described as the personality in action. The first essential to choice is that the person should perceive the possibility of choosing; he must have some realization of alternative possibilities or he cannot be said to have chosen. Sometimes he may perceive such possibilities where none exist, but more commonly he will fail to perceive them for a variety of reasons. He may lack the knowledge or the intelligence to see them, habit may so grip him that psychologically he is blind to alternatives most of the time, or he may vaguely see possibilities which he feels he cannot even consider; he must do

whatever it is. This last state is very common in neurotic conditions; extreme depression virtually excludes a whole lot of
actions which the person may see as intellectual possibilities
that have nothing to do with him. Guilt and anxiety can have
a like masking effect. Probably Rogers[12] has given the best
account of this sort of perceptual blinkering which so narrows
the seen possibilities for action that the individual is trapped
in a self-perpetuating cycle of unsatisfactory behaviour. Char-
acteristically, such people feel driven, feel captured by circumstances which block them on all sides, and feel a deep mistrust
of themselves whether consciously or unconsciously. They may
sometimes achieve a good deal, but more usually they are in
some degree ineffective as well as unhappy.

## Conflict

When faced with a choice this may be of a simple kind, that
is, it may involve only one value dimension and depend largely
on judgement on a given criterion. Such choices do not strictly
speaking arouse any conflict, though if the judgement is difficult
they may create confusion and arouse anxiety and, even in the
simplest cases, they involve a certain tension which is resolved
by the choice.

More often choices involve more than one value dimension
and choosing involves not only the evaluation of the situation
in terms of each of these, and a predictive judgement, but also
the ultimate weighing of these against each other. This arouses
a genuine conflict which characterizes much choice, though it
may not be of a proportion to distress the individual much. The
conflict can be extremely distressing if the matter is important,
the values nearly balanced and the outcome uncertain, in fact
it may become chronic, leaving the individual in some degree
of permanent distress. But this is not as common as one might
sometimes think.

[12] Rogers, C., *Client Centred Therapy*, Houghton Mifflin, Boston
(1951).

However, such unresolved conflicts can give rise to a number of abnormal states; they may be repressed, or otherwise excluded from consciousness, because of the pain they cause, and all hope of resolving them is then considerably decreased. This state arises typically when the immature organism is faced with a choice which it is incapable of making without some measure of self-destruction. Such situations also give rise to a pseudo-choice in which the person behaves in one way without giving up his impulse to behave in another. At the surface such "choices" give rise to vacillation, abrupt alterations in behaviour and general inconsistency; at a deeper level they create a measure of disintegration within the personality. The person resents and repudiates his choice, he does not really give up the alternative but hangs on to the possibility of having his cake and eating it. The better integrated the person the fewer of his choices will be like this, and the more deeply he will be committed to his chosen line of action. But considerable maturity is implied in the possibility of behaving in so wholehearted a manner. A person learns this capacity best in an environment which faces him only with the sort of choice he can reasonably cope with, which allows him to take decisions he can live with. One of the reasons why inconsistent treatment of children does them so much harm is that they fail to learn the way in which to handle decisions and their consequences. This does not mean that one cannot allow a child to change his mind if he makes a mistake and sees it, but rather that he should be given the opportunity to see quite clearly what is happening, and the measure of control that he has over himself and the situation. If this changes constantly he never manages to separate all this out and lives in a sort of magical world where chance is the main determinant of the outcome of his actions. In some measure the world is arbitrary, but not senseless. A magical view of the world may involve a lot of self reference, and a very rough handling of the idea of secondary causality. In such a world view disease may be a punishment, failure bad luck, and so on; the person never really works out the extent to

which he affects the world and it affects him. In a child of five
such reasoning is to be expected; but arbitrary self reference is
a limiting and immature state.

## Decision in action

From a great many of the laboratory studies and from
theoretical discussions one may get the impression that choices
are typically between clearly presented alternatives, but this is
a somewhat distorted view. While many choices are of this
kind, a great many more are experienced as "whether to do X"
with only vague alternatives. Given a possibility, it may seem
to the person as just an opportunity to do what he wants; he
does not perhaps feel he has to choose at all, he goes ahead
and does it because it is possible. But usually a possibility
offered to an individual really makes it necessary for him to
envisage, however vaguely, a whole host of alternatives; he
chooses whether to do X against this background of alternatives which have varying degrees of possibility. He decides
whether he will go to the cinema more than he decides whether
he will look at television or do the washing up. This means that
he may not take into account at the time some of the consequences of his choice, since the alternatives he considers must
be limited by the time and energy he has available for making
up his mind. Often he may be dismayed by its consequences
and repine considerably along the lines "if only I had known".
Again, while some measure of this reaction is common to all
of us and indeed proper, it can give rise to a frame of mind in
which the individual is not prepared to face up to the consequences of his choice, the far off hills grow greener and greener,
and the "if only" frame of mind chronic. Such an attitude
cripples the capacity for effective action and reduces the person's sense of responsibility, and makes him inclined to
attribute this to other people and events rather than to himself. In the same way some degree of responsibility can be shed
by following the "rules" provided by others; these may be
designed in the first place to create order in society, to keep

things on an even keel, to make life easier for everyone; but they can take a vicious hold on the personality so that all sense of independence and responsibility is lost, they can become virtually an alternative to living. The Nuremberg trials provide a lasting warning to those who equate blind obedience with responsible human action.

The free person, then, is essentially one who knows what he is doing, who understands himself well enough to know what he wants and values. He is a person who takes the responsibility for his decisions and actions and is prepared to live with the consequences. He is not a person who is free from conflicts, or who never makes mistakes, but who makes use of these in the constant endeavour to make the best use of the opportunities which life offers him.

# CHAPTER VI

# PSYCHOLOGICAL DETERMINISM AND HUMAN FREEDOM

The question of personal freedom and responsibility has always been a vexed one, but while it was once largely the concern of religion, law and philosophy, now a new element has been added by psychology in the last hundred years. This has proved difficult to assimilate, leaving people with a general impression that psychological reasoning has changed things, but unclear about how much notice to take of it, or even of what they are supposed to take notice. The ordinary person is in fact being offered, by a variety of specialists, several different versions of responsibility, quite apart from his own views on the subject. The result is confusing, particularly as each view is strongly argued as the one he "ought" to take notice of. His aunt has kleptomania, he is told, so that he must not blame her if she takes the teaspoons, but it is quite definitely his fault if his child picks flowers in the park; on the other hand his ulcer troubles him because he is maladjusted, which is the fault of the kleptomaniac aunt who brought him up so badly; he feels responsible because a brick fell off his house and knocked over a passer-by, but was quite happy coveting his neighbour's television set until someone told him that it was a sin; if at this point the poor man decides that it is probably all fate, the atom bomb, or the government, and nothing to do with him, it is not surprising.

At the same time a great many people are increasingly aware that psychology has developed in a way which opens the door to a new type of coercion through the manipulation of people in a nice scientific way. So that on the one hand psychology has been responsible for the suggestion of inherent limits to man's freedom and, on the other, for discovering methods to take it away if he still has it. I do not propose to deal with this second problem here, because it creates a moral problem only if we can establish some real meaning to psychological freedom, and thus arrive at a context in which the moral use of psychological techniques can interest us.[1]

Psychologists themselves have been well aware of the determinist implications of their science ever since the end of the last century when psychology began to be important as an experimental study. William James wrestled with the problem for many years and came in the end to the conclusion that psychological determinism of a kind which denied any freedom or responsibility to the individual was untenable. Although he enjoyed so considerable a reputation on both sides of the Atlantic, this view never caught the popular imagination in the way that the more luridly determinist theories of later writers have done. One effect of the widespread determinism of some now classical psychologies is that a whole lot of people have plunged into the discussion and helped to confuse the issues involved still further. It may be worthwhile to glance at these before we look at the more central arguments.

In particular, the growing concern in psychology with prediction has led some people to confuse predictability and

---

[1] In passing it may be worthwhile to point out that the less radical of these techniques appear to work effectively only when the person is not alerted to them; and the more radical so damage the person that though he may appear to behave normally he has ceased to be in any real sense himself (just as the person who has suffered gross neurological damage often ceases to be recognizably himself, although he continues to behave "normally" in many respects).

freedom; since psychologists themselves seem to make this mistake, it should not surprise us that philosophers, physicists and other interested parties do the same thing. In this context it is suggested that an action which is predictable cannot be free; conversely that if one can show that an action is not predictable then it may be free. Now the most unpredictable events are random or chance events; this logically means, if the predictable is determined, that randomness is the only form of freedom. To equate "freedom" with randomness is to suggest that the less predictable a person is the freer he is. The person's freedom, however, can hardly reside in someone else's inability to predict what he is going to do next; either it is proper to him, and not the observer, or it is largely irrelevant. Very simple organisms are highly predictable in their responses because these are few in number and the stimuli they respond to equally limited; the limitation of their freedom lies not in their predictability, but in their inherent structure. Where behaviour has a wider range of possibilities it may be less "predictable" just because the observer has greater difficulty in taking the relevant factors into account. When we come to people, negative predictions are easier than positive ones. We can be fairly sure that a particular person because of his limitations will not do certain things because he lacks the capacity; but this will not get us very far because, within his capacity, the remaining possibilities are bewilderingly great.

It is possible, however, with adults whose personality is well integrated, to achieve a high level of correct prediction as to their actions and reactions simply because they display coherence and consistency, and when our prediction goes wrong we can usually understand the nature of our error because their behaviour makes sense. From one point of view the better organized the person is, the easier it is to "predict" what he will do; and the more we understand of him, the better we shall do. Looked at in this light we can see that it is typically the insane who are for most people unpredictable, although this is usually because we do not understand why they do what they

do. It would be ridiculous to argue that this degree of un-
predictability conferred on them a greater degree of freedom
than others possess, since we much more usually decide that
such people are not in any meaningful sense free, that they
cannot be said to be responsible for what they do.

The freest people may well be among the most predictable
precisely because they know what they are doing and why they
are doing it; they know what matters most to them, they do not
vacillate and they are not shifted by every wind that blows and
they are not at war with themselves. So that predictability
cannot, in any sense, solve the problem of psychological determinism, although it may tell us something about the person
or the skill of the predictor. It is also possible to side-step the
issue by taking refuge in cybernetics and neuro-physiology,
arguing hotly either that the principles of cybernetics show that
we are completely determined or, equally hotly, that the uncertainty principle lets us all out. Entertaining as all this may
be, it is all rather irrelevant, because psychology is not neuro-
physiology and cybernetics is something we have made up, not
something that made us up. We should concern ourselves with
the person, in whom after all we are interested. It is, however,
easy to understand why people become involved in such
peripheral discussion; the real problem is too difficult, too
involved, and unlikely to give us the kind of certainty one way
or the other that we so much prefer when we can get it.

If we avoid these sterile side tracks, what can we say of
human freedom? First we can be quite clear that, if it exists, it
exists within strict limits. These limits are initially very obvious
and acceptable, but, as we come closer to the deeply personal,
are less self-evident. We have already seen that we are limited
by our species characteristics, by our size and our shape, our
long immaturity, our needs and wants: these are the limits that
we all share. In addition, since we grow up within a culture,
and since that culture provides us with the framework in which
we learn all our human skills, our language, interpersonal rôles
and appropriate social conduct, and the form of our intellectual

life, it limits us inevitably—it also, of course, gives us the pattern of our humanity. In any time or place culture itself is limited, and we are more or less bounded by these shared limits; it is only with difficulty and even pain and guilt that we move far away from our cultural origins. That is not the end of it; we are further, during our long period of growth, subject to individual experiences which mould us inescapably; they make us what we are and exclude what we might have been for good or ill. We learn ways of dealing with experience which can hamper us because they limit our self-knowledge and generally make us less than we might have been; equally in more fortunate circumstances they may allow us to develop to the best of our full potential. One may well ask at this point what else is left. It seems to me that we are left with what matters, although I readily see that others feel we are so over-whelmingly formed by species, culture and early experience that the rest is silence.

Yet we can reflect on all that has formed us, we can know our limitations; this is the beginning of our personal freedom, the capacity for reflective evaluation of our own determinism. The core of our freedom seems to rest in our capacity for choice as well as judgement and reflection; in this sense any animal is free, but the freedom of an animal, like that of a young child or a mentally retarded person, is fixed within the limits of his understanding. Morality demands an understanding of the ethical, just as the pursuit of truth demands a value for it as something understood, or the appreciation of beauty some idea of the beautiful. Precisely because and when and how we know the meaning of these ideas we can apply them relevantly to our lives; they become a "deciding factor" in our choices. Without that understanding we should, strictly speaking, be no less free, but our freedom would mean something less, not merely something different.

It is not impulsiveness, nor randomness, nor changeableness that expresses our freedom, but the coherence which self-awareness, long term goals and stable values, will give to our lives. It is arguable that for many the limitations that arise from nature and growth will virtually remove all possibility of freedom; that we can know this, even know it of ourselves and worry about it, means that psychological freedom is within our grasp in some measure if not actually in our grip. We enjoy enough of it to value it, to work for it in ourselves and others; in doing just this we exercise the freedom we aspire to. It is, I think, palpably true that some of us are freer than others, but probably each of us has our own measure of freedom, even if in some, youth, illness, intellectual retardation or extremes of deprivation and duress may rob it of much moral significance.

It may perhaps be argued that such a view is mere wishful thinking in view of the rigidly determinist standpoint adopted by many psychologists. It may be useful to look at some of the most extreme of these views a little more closely to see what they actually amount to. Outstanding among those who have forced a popular revision of the idea of moral responsibility are the writings of Freud and to a lesser extent those of Adler. Jung's theoretical formulations, although in some respects more extreme than those of Freud, were less critical for two reasons: one, that he argued quite explicitly for the principle of self-determination in the process of individuation and, secondly, because, unlike Freud, he was neither atheistic nor anti-religious. In fact, of course, his theory presents considerable difficulties for a theory of self-determination, since his idea of the individual as a sort of expression of the collective soul or manifestation of the *zeitgeist* make the determining agents external to the individual in a manner much more radical than anything Freud suggested. However that may be, Freud's explicit concern with psychological determinism, and perhaps even more his militant atheism, make him a central figure in the modification of contemporary ideas about psychological determinism. Partly, this undoubtedly is due to the near religious fervour with which many people in the 1920's and '30's took to psychoanalysis as a system of belief, taking the idea of psychological determinism to extremes which Freud would never have accepted. The anomalous side of this is that in all the excitement people seem to have lost sight of the avowed aim of psychoanalytic treatment, which is directly aimed at increasing the person's capacity for rational self-determination.

It is true that Freud, with a pessimism that is understandable both in terms of his own temperament and the general behaviour of the human race, was gloomy about the possibilities for insight, rationality and conscious control of behaviour. But even if he argued that repression was the price we paid for civilization, and our capacity for self-delusion nearly endless, he did nevertheless also argue that in the search for truth and rationality lay the proper goal of science and of humanity. There may well be a certain inconsistency in his point of view which he never really resolved, but in considering what he meant by psychic determinism it is quite improper to attribute to him views which, while perhaps more consistent, were not in fact his own.

In such widely read works as the *Psychopathology of Everyday Life*[2] Freud argued that there is no such thing as a random psychic event, that things which we class as mistakes, slips of the tongue or pen, are often in fact meaningful. Equally he argued that dreams and phantasy are meaningful rather than chaotic, but that such meaning is hidden in elaborate symbolism. Psychic determinism in this sense merely reduces what might be called the random in human experience and behaviour, and this seems eminently acceptable. By a similar type of argument Freud suggested that neurotic and psychotic symptoms were "determined" in terms of early and forgotten experiences and desires; that while consciously inexplicable, they were in fact loaded with psychological meaning and maintained by unconscious motivation. He later extended such arguments[3] to cover other aspects of behaviour which we would ordinarily think of as "reasonable" and explicable, suggesting that hidden motives incongruous with conscious attitudes lay behind these;

[2] 1920, London, Fisher Unwin.
[3] For example, in *The Future of an Illusion*, Hogarth, London (1934).

again he argued that such behaviour made sense, but added that here the "real" sense was different from the apparent. Since the person was unaware of the hidden motive he could not be considered as responsible in the classic sense. To explain the processes of unconscious motivation Freud developed a theory of personality which greatly emphasized the importance of the early years of life. This theory involved the postulate that in ordinary people early desires and experiences had become repressed in the process whereby the conscience (or Super-ego) was formed, and that these desires and motives of the child continued to exert a pressure to action of which the individual was no longer aware. Since he was unaware of them, they were little modified by later experience. Such a theory has many difficulties, which have in the years since it was formulated been exhaustively discussed on all sides. Particularly, the strong historical bias has been widely criticized even among those who accepted a great part of the theory; among the so called neo-Freudians people like Karen Horney[4] have held that later events are much more formative and important than Freud allows.

As far as the theory of psychological determinism goes Freud's main contentions were that all behaviour and experience is meaningful and determined precisely by past events, and further that many aspects of behaviour are determined by deeply unconscious motives over which the individual has no control and into which he has no insight. In popular thought, then, early traumas and the unconscious largely replaced heredity and "glands" as the framework of a strong scientific determinism. Since they were more flexible, more pervasive and in some sense more demonstrable, they presented a much more serious challenge to the notion of self-determination and responsibility than the earlier theories.

Perhaps the most insidious aspect of such psychic de-

[4] In, for example, such books as *The Neurotic Personality of our Time*, Routledge & Kegan Paul, London (1937), or *Our Inner Conflicts*, Norton, New York (1945).

terminism is the threat which it offers to the very processes of argument themselves; once rationalization is admitted, it gives rise to a degree of uncertainty about the process whereby it is demonstrated. The idea that people could be deceived about themselves was not a novel one when Freud wrote, but his insistence on the critical importance of infancy and childhood and the strength and extent of unconscious determinants, gave the problem raised by such self-deception a new importance. Along with a new insight into the limitations against which the person had to struggle in his attempt to achieve rationality, we obviously had a reaction in which these efforts have been seen as so puny that for practical purposes we might as well resign ourselves to the view that people "cannot help themselves," the curious thing being perhaps that some of the most ardent proponents of this view have evidently felt a great sense of personal responsibility for either freeing people from their re-pressions or shielding them from blame. To argue that anyone should not "blame" another, that he should realize the other is not responsible, is to invest that one person at least with some sort of moral responsibility.

This is perhaps best demonstrated in another view of psycho-logical determinism that owes little or nothing to Freud. Inspired in the first place by Pavlov's work, behaviourist psychologists from Watson onwards have assumed a complete determinism as a postulate. Since they have deliberately ex-cluded the dimension of experience from the study of psychology, what people think is of no concern to them. Un-like Freud who devoted much of his working life to attempts to give people some degree of genuine self-determination, the behaviourists have devoted themselves to the control of be-haviour through learning. In suggesting that they could, in theory, make anyone do or be anything they liked, through a suitable process of conditioning, some of them have allowed a limit, in the shape of areas of psychology which are beyond their scope; but others have admitted no such limitations—all is controllable.

Novels such as *Brave New World* and *1984* probe the logical outcome of such claims and attempt to deal with the problem of what we might call outer-determinism. Most behaviourist psychologists have refrained from any deep reflection on the problem of psychological determinism, and have perhaps failed to see what the novelists have grasped, that the system assumes a determiner, someone outside the system—a free Big Brother in a world where everyone else is determined.

Exceptionally, Skinner[5] in his illuminating novel *Walden Two*[6] does recognize this necessity for at least one responsible individual. In his scientific, as opposed to his imaginative, writing he fails to really explore this; he suggests that, through a process known as "operant conditioning", anyone can be made to do anything you want. The reason why his novel is more interesting than his more orthodox reflections is that experiments demonstrating the range of remarkable accomplishments acquired by a starving hen (they call it 80 per cent body weight, it sounds nicer) trapped in a little box pressing levers or tapping panels in a complicated way for small rewards, may show us how completely the behaviour of a starving hen can be controlled by a well-fed psychologist. But since she has singularly little freedom anyway in that situation, to be able to limit this still further, while interesting, is not felt to be a matter of near personal threat.

But Skinner has concerned himself with the future of the human race and feels its only hope of survival lies in being conditioned to what I think we may very reasonably call a more moral way of life.[7] His concern is benevolent in intention, the celebrated "teaching machine" his most conspicuous contribution towards the preferred Utopia. In *Walden Two* he

---

[5] Professor of Psychology at Harvard University and one of the leading American experimental psychologists; he is interested mainly in learning and allied subjects.

[6] Skinner, B. F., *Walden Two*, Macmillan, New York (1948).

[7] Skinner, B. F., *Cumulative Record*, Appleton-Century Crofts, New York (1959).

imagines a small world in which, through scientific control of the environment from birth, an amiable, co-operative, creative group of people live in an earthly paradise. They experience no anti-social urges, they want only the right, the proper and the sensible. It sounds lovely; but the interest lies in the treatment of the creator of this Paradise, who alone cannot fit into this world because (though the author certainly does not put it this way) he "knows sin" and is capable of anger, envy, boredom and remorse. While the whole tenor of the book suggests that he is less successfully human than his products, in fact the author cannot help but make him somehow much more important and significant than they are. The reason for this seems to be that he could have made a good world or a bad one, and chose to make a good one, while the others never make any such moral choice, because they cannot be confronted with it. Thus the hero is the only person in the system with any moral freedom.

The most curious episode of the whole book is that in which, with a somewhat selfconscious and obvious symbolism, the hero goes up a hill and sits on a white stone, shaped like a throne, and surveys his "creation". He feels it to be good. Thus the hero, although he is sad because he is not "good" like the inhabitants of *Walden Two*, identifies himself with God as creator and so enjoys a degree of superiority over them—a superiority which appears to have its roots in a capacity for free moral choice.

Perhaps wisely, most psychologists do not write novels which would enable us to explore the personal philosophical context in which their theories of psychological determinism rest. This novel of Skinner's underlines what one suspects is true of others, that they operate within a philosophical contradiction of the kind already suggested. It is always the other people who are determined from without or within and who lack a capacity for meaningful moral choice. They must shelve in some curious way the contradiction between the philosophical system they live by and the one to which they are theoretically committed in their psychology, by keeping them well separated.[8]

Clearly then an easy assumption of psychological determinism fails to satisfy even its most ardent exponents, although a superficial reading of many psychological texts would suggest that it is a self-evident truth that moral freedom is a figment of the fevered imagination of suffering humanity.

Psychological freedom for these determinists then resides in rationality, choice and human concern, just as it must for all of us; only I can see no reason why psychologists should be supposed to be the only people who enjoy such God-like attributes. It may be useful to sum up the minimal conditions for such free action, so that we can see precisely where all this discussion has taken us. The person, to act freely, must perceive some alternatives which he can differentiate successfully; he must be able to predict with some measure of accuracy what the outcome of his action is likely to be; he must be able to apply the relevant criteria meaningfully to the situation; and finally he must know enough of his own wishes, needs and desires in the face of the alternatives to allow that steadiness of purpose which characterizes psychological maturity.

If any of these conditions is not fulfilled then there is no real choice, whatever the situation appears to be like to anyone else. This leaves us with one final dilemma: if we want to talk specifically of moral freedom and moral responsibility, how does the person arrive at his idea of the "good"? There are obviously many possible answers to this, but he must of necessity find that idea partly in what he is himself, partly in the social world in which he lives, and partly in his intellectual struggle to understand his place in nature, history and society. Ultimately the Christian finds his idea of the "good" in Revelation, which is part of both history and society; but that

---

[8] In Watson's famous dictum, "Give me a dozen healthy infants, well formed.... I'll guarantee to take any one at random and train him to become any type of specialist I might select..." etc. (page 104, *Behaviourism*, 1931 edn.), we see the Achilles' heel—why him?

idea is one which he, like anyone else, must understand through learning, listening, thinking and personal experience, although his acceptance of it rests in faith.

# SELECT BIBLIOGRAPHY

*In this series:* Biot, René: *What is Life?*; Dominian, J.: *Psychiatry and the Christian*; Le Trocquer, René: *What is Man?*

Allport, G. W.: *The Individual and his Religion*, London, Constable, and New York, Macmillan, 1951; *Pattern and Growth in Personality*, London, Constable, and New York, Holt, 1961.

Arnold, M.: *The Human Person*, New York, Ronald Press, 1954.

Bowlby, J.: *Child Care and the Growth of Love*, Harmondsworth and Baltimore, Penguin, 1956.

Brown, R.: *Words and Things*, Glencoe, Ill., Free Press, 1958.

Harding, D. W.: *Social Psychology and Individual Values*, London, Hutchinson, and New York, Rinehart, 1953.

Hebb, D. O.: *A Textbook of Psychology*, London, Saunders, and New York, Wiley, 1958.

Johnson, D. M.: *The Psychology of Thought and Judgement*, New York, Harper, 1955.

Lorenz, K.: *King Solomon's Ring*, London, Methuen, and New York, Crowell, 1952.

Maslow, A. H.: *Motivation and Personality*, London, Hamish Hamilton, and New York, Harper, 1954.

Piaget, J.: *The Moral Judgment of the Child*, London, Kegan Paul, and Glencoe, Ill., Free Press, 1932.

Skinner, B. F.: *Cumulative Record*, London, Methuen, 1959, and New York, Appleton, 1958.

Suttie, I.: *Origins of Love and Hate*, London, Kegan Paul, and New York, Julian, 1935.

Thorpe, W. H.: *Learning and Instinct in Animals*, London, Methuen, 1963.

Whiting, J. W., and Child, I. R.: *Child Training and Personality*, New Haven, Conn., Yale Univ. Press, 1953.